CONTENTS

1
Ossie the Pop Star

Ossie Osgood was doing his music practice. There was only half an hour to go before his weekly lesson, so naturally he was very busy.

"This stupid tape recorder," he said, giving it a kick. "I bet that Lucy's been at it. I bet she's pinched the batteries and put in her old ones. I know her. Just the rotten trick she would play."

At last he got the machine to work. He inserted a tape and switched it on.

"Here we are, ladies and gentlemen," said Ossie, putting on his best Radio 4 announcer's voice. "Here is your very own Ossie Osgood, star of stage, screen and seven violin lessons, playing you a selection of his favourite scales. Thank you . . ."

Ossie turned the volume up, opened his bedroom door, listened carefully to make sure his mother down below could hear, then with two leaps he was across his bedroom, doing his special long jump, as seen on TV by Daley Thompson, and landing with a crash on his bed.

He listened again, then picked up an old Spurs programme, which he had read five times already. He kept it on the right-hand side of his bed, always available in case he had to fill in an odd moment when he might be caught by sudden boredom or by sudden exhaustion, such as after two minutes of violin practice.

On the left-hand side of his bed he had his secret bag of sweets, hidden in case his mother or, even worse, his younger sister Lucy should find them. Ossie needed them near him, in case of sudden depression.

As he read the programme, and ate his sweets, he found himself, now and again, humming along with the scales.

"Ossie Osgood! What on earth are you doing?"

It was his mother. She had come up the stairs so quietly that he hadn't heard.

"What a fright!" he said. "You nearly gave me a

8

heart attack. I can feel the cholesterol rushing all over my body . . ."

"Why are you lying on your bed?" She listened for a few moments, looked round the bedroom, then walked over to the tape recorder and switched it off.

"You're only cheating yourself," she said. "Pretending it was you practising. I might have known you weren't doing your lessons."

"Whatcha mean?" said Ossie, indignantly. "It *was* me playing. Doesn't sound like Yehudi Manure, does it? Can't you tell the difference? Mr Peabody told me to make a tape of me playing, then listen to it and read the notes, then I'd be able to spot the mistakes. See, clever clogs. It *is* part of my lessons . . ."

"So why are you studying those photographs of White Hart Lane?"

"What?" said Ossie, surreptitiously putting his hand on the floor, searching around till he found his music book. It was lying half under his bed, exactly where he'd thrown it when he returned from last week's lesson. "I had a headache with all the practising, so I just took a short break. Mr

9

Peabody said never practise with a headache . . ."

His mother got hold of Ossie by the arm and forced him off the bed.

"Gerroff, that hurts, woman. You know I haven't got strong arms. Not fair. That's why it tires me so much, playing that stupid violin."

"Right," said his mother. "I'm going to sit here and watch you till it's time to go for your lesson."

Ossie had never wanted to learn the violin. There were very few things he did want to do in life, apart from learning to play more football and better snooker, drive a car, eat more sweets, spend money, read comics, play computer games or watch television. At the age of twelve, he was quite good at most of those things already. It was learning lessons he was not so keen on.

"I hate this violin," he said, picking it up. "Doesn't even fit me."

Ossie was so small and weedy that even with a three-quarters size violin he had to play with a special pad under his neck. His mother had made him one and covered it with black velvet. Ossie maintained it made him itch. In fact, everything to do with the violin made him itch.

He propped his music book on his music stand, turning to lesson three, which was a difficult manoeuvre, as he was still holding the violin under his chin.

"Oh, don't help," he shouted to his mother.

Ossie gave the stand a kick, and immediately it collapsed, turning itself into a pile of metal bones on the floor, like one of those puzzles you get in Christmas crackers which are impossible to unfold.

"Now look what you've done," he said. "All your fault. I can't do any practising now."

His mother patiently set up the music stand again and stood beside him this time till he started at last to play lesson three.

"You could be quite good, if only you practised," she said, as she listened to him. "Mr Peabody said so last week. He's been so kind and patient. Taken such trouble over you. I'm sure he's organized this orchestral trip specially for you."

"Oh no, it's not today, is it?" said Ossie, groaning.

"You know it's straight after your lesson, and

he's only taking four of his pupils. You should be very grateful."

"Huh," said Ossie. "Anyway, I've got to rest now, Mum. Honest. My arms are sore."

"That's because you're not used to it. If you practised more often, your arms wouldn't feel tired."

"Not just me arms. Me legs are tired as well. All this standing. If only you'd let me play the drums, this wouldn't have happened. You sit to play the drums. Much easier."

"I'm waiting, Oswald."

"Nobody else in my class goes to rotten music lessons any more. Dez has given up the trumpet. His mum let him. You're the only mother who forces people."

"I don't care what other people do. You're carrying on for the rest of this term. Then we might think about it."

Ossie played a few bars, and then stopped once again, making a face.

"It's this stupid music, all these boring scales and soppy little tunes by people with funny names.

Who ever heard of anyone called Sherbert? No wonder they write stupid tunes, with stupid names like that."

"Mr Peabody has already told you," said his mother. "As soon as you finish this book, he's going to get you a selection of Beatles tunes. Won't that be lovely?"

"Yuck, Beatles," said Ossie, making an even worse face. He knew his mother loved the Beatles. She was always saying how no one wrote tunes like theirs any more.

"They're ancient," said Ossie. "They're from the Dark Ages."

"They happen to have written many modern classics," said his mother. "And they knew how to sing songs properly as well."

"Ugh, that Paul McCartney. Load of rubbish."

He knew that Paul was his mother's favourite, always had been. She smiled, ignoring his insult, waiting for him to start again.

"Hold on," said Ossie, suddenly putting down his violin, this time very defiantly. "In that book about them, what you've got, what you've always got your nose in, it says they didn't have no music lessons. They taught themselves. So why are you forcing me, eh?"

"Right," said his mother, looking at her watch. "You can stop now and get ready. I don't want you being late, not today."

"Got you there, huh," said Ossie. "Sussed you out."

Lucy was in the living room, doing her scales on the piano. She hardly looked up when Ossie came into the room.

"What was all that screeching upstairs?" she said.

"Mum," said Ossie. "Her voice always sounds like that. She should oil it some time."

Mrs Osgood handed Ossie his anorak and his violin case, standing in front of him to make sure he had everything.

"Here's the money for the train. Now don't forget to thank Mr Peabody for taking you to see the orchestra."

"Thank him. Huh."

"I don't expect you back till quite late," said his mother. "Lucy and I will probably go shopping.

Now do try and enjoy it, please."

"I think my hand is stuck in my pocket," said Ossie, struggling with his trousers.

"Don't start that again."

"No, really, you never believe anything I say. I really think I have."

Mrs Osgood pulled Ossie's hand out of his pocket and pushed him to the front door, which wasn't hard. Ossie was so very small and slight. Almost anyone could push him around.

"Who's that at the front window?" said Ossie, suddenly. "Lucy, I think it's someone for you?"

Lucy got up from the piano to look out of the window. As she did so, Ossie leaned over and gave a very sharp twist to her piano stool, sending it round and round, making it lower and lower. It was a trick he had spent a long time practising, when he should have been practising other things, such as his violin. He had also oiled the seat, so it not only went down quickly, but very quietly.

"I knew you were lying," said Lucy. "There's nobody there."

She sat down again, but the seat was now so low that she landed on the floor.

"I thought you were playing the piano, Lucy," said Ossie, opening the front door. "Not playing on the carpet . . ."

Ossie started off at a fast pace, just in case Lucy or his mother came after him. Gradually, he slowed down, thinking about the lesson with Mr Peabody ahead, and the trip to hear the orchestra. Then he quickened up again when he realized he was going to pass Flossie Teacake's house. She was in his class and he certainly didn't want her to see him carrying his soppy violin.

As he got near her house, he saw a curtain twitch at an upstairs window he knew was Flossie's bedroom. She must be spying on him.

"Grrr, grrr, boom, boom," said Ossie, pointing his violin case upwards, as if it was a tommygun, spraying her whole house with bullets.

The window opened and Flossie's fat arm came out, giving him a fat, friendly wave.

"Stupid girl," said Ossie, putting his violin under his anorak. "Can't she see I'm a gangster?"

"Oh Ossie, we've been trying for ages to get you."

It was Mrs Peabody, looking very worried and agitated, standing at her front gate.

Ossie didn't hear her at first. He was walking at his slowest, dragging his feet along, head down, his shoulders hunched.

"I think your phone must be out of order."

"What? Phone? Not my fault. Just came to pieces when I tried to mend it, not my fault . . ."

"Mr Peabody has been taken ill and he's had to cancel your lesson and the visit to the orchestra. I know you'll be terribly disappointed. Please apologize to your mother."

" 'S'all right," said Ossie. "I'll tell her."

"But we'll expect you at the same time next week, for your normal lesson. I'm sure Mr Peabody will be better by then. It will give you another whole week to do your practising."

Ossie turned away with a scowl and walked back up the street.

"Huh, I'm exhausted as it is," thought Ossie. "Having it hanging over me all week. Very tiring, not practising. Now I've got to not practise the same stuff for another whole week . . ."

"Hello, Grandad. It's me."

Ossie had let himself into his grandfather's home, a little flat in a modern block of Sheltered Housing for senior citizens. Ossie had his own key, as he was supposed to make regular visits and do any bits of shopping that might be required.

"Grandad! It's me."

"I didn't think it was Al Capone," said his grandad.

"Shall I make you a cup of tea?" said Ossie.

He went into the little living room, put down his violin, and switched on the kettle.

"You've finished early," said Grandad. "What time is it, anyway?"

"I was so good," said Ossie, "Mr Peabody said I could leave early. I am his prize pupil. May I have one of your digestives?"

"Certainly not, they're counted."

"OK then, I'll have a Mint Imperial. I know where you hide them."

"When I was a lad, you could leave all doors unlocked, no bolts on windows, no burglar alarms."

"When you were a lad," said Ossie, "I thought you all lived in caves."

"Watch it, you, or you'll get the back of my hand. OK, you can have one digestive. But go easy on the butter."

They sat and had tea together, and digestives, with lashings of butter.

"She says it's poison," said Ossie.

"Who does?"

"Mum. She won't let us have butter on anything."

Grandad got up and switched on the TV, without the sound. He preferred it that way, making

19

his own commentary. He considered all commentators half-witted, or big-headed, or both.

"Grandad," said Ossie. "When you were a boy, did you have to go to music lessons?"

"When I was your age, son, I was in the army."

"Don't be daft, they didn't take boys of twelve and three-quarters in the army."

"I lied about my age," said Grandad.

Ossie had no reply to that. He knew that Grandad still lied about his age, saying he was sixty-nine, when Old Ma Pigg, his neighbour, said he was eighty.

Ossie had gone through life so far wishing he was *older* than he was. Not younger. But it would be no use him lying. No one would believe him.

"Thanks for the tea," he said, getting up. "I'm not allowed two sugars at home. Or even one sugar. Or even tea. All we get is water and dry bread. Bye."

Instead of letting himself out of his grandad's front door, Ossie opened it, then closed it loudly. He listened carefully to the shouts of Grandad talking to the television, then very slowly he opened the door of Grandad's bedroom.

Ossie was not supposed to go in there. It was private property, highly secret, Government issue, so Grandad always said. But something rather strange had happened the last time Ossie had managed to sneak into it. He wondered if it would happen again.

The bedroom was like a little museum, but totally disorganized and overcrowded with wartime relics, bundles of old newspapers, parcels of clothing, letters and documents. On the walls were uniforms and medals. On the dusty shelves were what looked like real daggers.

Ossie made his way towards a large, old-fashioned wardrobe in the corner, climbing over boxes and packing cases. He opened the door of the wardrobe and at once he could smell a powerful, musty, fusty smell. Mothballs, probably. Perhaps even gunpowder.

He stepped inside. The door creaked and slowly closed behind him. It was almost dark, except for a few chinks of light coming through some cracks in the wooden panels at the back of the wardrobe.

With his hands, Ossie could feel some old uniforms. He made out the shape of the badges and ribbons, then the cold leather of what might be boots, or a gun holster.

Ossie was searching and feeling for something very special, a large, heavy leather belt with a huge ornamental buckle. He knew it was enormous, big enough to go twice if not three times round his little, weedy waist, but he knew he had to put it on.

"Oh, if only I was eighteen now, this very moment," said Ossie, closing his eyes, wishing very hard. "It's not fair. I want to be grown up now, big and strong, tall and old . . ."

Ossie's body started to shake, as if it was somehow moving. He felt dizzy and the world seemed to be going up and up in a magical lift.

When he opened his eyes, several remarkable things had happened. For a start, the belt now fitted properly.

Ossie stood outside the wardrobe and looked at himself in the mirror. He could see before him a tall, well built young man of eighteen, broad-shouldered, strong-armed, possibly even in need of a shave.

He smiled, and the face of an eighteen-year-old smiled back at him.

★

Oz was on the London train. He had decided he would go for the day after all. Now that he was eighteen, he didn't need to be taken, or go in a party of weedy, soppy twelve-year-olds. He could do what he liked. Go where he liked.

As the train drew into Euston, Oz got up from his seat, and gave himself a crack on the head. It didn't hurt, much, now that he was so strong and tough. "I forgot I was so tall. Haven't got used to that yet."

A party of Girl Guides were struggling to open the door, shouting for their Guider to come and help.

"No problem," said Oz, striding through the carriage. "I often find that young people do have trouble with these doors."

"There is no need," said the Guider, pushing her way through the group of Guides. "We can manage, thank you very much."

"Miss Turkey!" Oz let out a little moan. He hadn't recognized her in her Guide uniform. At weekends, she ran a pack of Guides. On school days, she was the teacher in charge of Ossie's class.

23

Oz tried to back away and hide from her, but she stared straight through him, unaware that she had ever seen him before.

"How did you know my name is Miss Turkey?" she asked. "I don't know you, do I?"

"What?" said Oz. "No, I said, 'Missed the key'. Not Miss Turkey. I think your girls missed the key of the door. Here. Let me try."

Oz hardly seemed to touch the handle, when the door flew open. He and a pile of Guides fell out, with Miss Turkey on top of them. As Oz stood up, he found the handle had come away in his hand.

"I didn't realize I was that strong," he said. "Just call me Superman."

"Here, you," shouted a voice. "What are you doing messing about with that door?"

A ticket inspector was coming towards Oz, looking rather angry.

"You do look vaguely familiar after all," said Miss Turkey.

"Gotta go," said Oz. "Have a nice day out in London. Don't get lost . . ."

Oz ran along the platform, then stopped, realizing

he might get lost, being in London on his own.

"No chance," he said to himself. "How can I, when I'm eighteen?"

The inspector and two porters came rushing towards him, so Oz quickly jumped on the back of a luggage trolley, and using it like a skateboard, he whizzed to the end of the platform and up a short ramp to the ticket barrier.

"Tickets please," said a voice from a little cabin.

Oz went through in a flash, so quickly that nobody stopped him.

Right across the concourse went Oz, scattering piles of luggage, just managing to miss a crowd of very noisy, rowdy football supporters. He banged through them, turning and twisting his trolley like a downhill skier in order not to touch any. Then he noticed they were Arsenal fans.

He kept on going, getting up even greater speed, down into the underground car park, round past the taxis, then back up another ramp. He was now approaching the Arsenal fans from a different direction, catching them completely unawares. This time he wasn't quite so careful. Quite a few, alas, got knocked over.

"Terribly sorry," said Oz.

As they picked themselves up, they could faintly hear in the distance the voice of the Runaway Trolley leaving Euston Station. It appeared to be singing, "Glory, Glory, Hallelujah, Spurs go marching on . . ."

Oz was staring into the window of a shop in Charing Cross Road. He had read in one of his comics that this was the area for instruments and music.

"Oh, if only I had the money," he said. "I know I could play them really well, now that I'm eighteen. But how can I afford them?

"Perhaps I'll try Kettle Street next, or is it Teapot Lane, or Frying Pan Place? Something like that. Might be cheaper there."

It was a set of drums he was admiring most, longing to get his hands on them.

"Who'd want to play a soppy violin? Just think of the noise I could make with them."

The shop door opened and out came four young men, all dressed in colourful stage clothes, silks and satins with tight trousers and very large, ornate, diamond-encrusted belts. They were just

about to climb into a large limousine which had
drawn up.

" 'Scuse me," said Oz. "Could you tell me the
way to Tinpot Alley?"

"You mean Tin Pan Alley," said one of them,
and all the others laughed.

"That's it," said Oz. "I usually get my drums
there."

"You a drummer?" said another of the four.

"The best in our class," said Oz. "I mean the
best in any class, the world, the hemisphere."

The one who appeared to be the leader was look-ing at Oz very carefully, studying his clothes.

"You should hear me on the desk tops," said Oz, "when Miss is out of the room . . ."

"Don't think I know them," said the leader.

"It's the name of our group," said Oz, hurriedly. "The Screaming Desk Tops. We're going to be very big one day, if any of us ever get to be big, or even eighteen . . ."

The group all laughed with Oz this time, rather than at him.

"He's not bad, is he?" said the leader, turning to the rest of his group. "That fool Ziggy is obviously completely lost or smashed . . ."

"You mean he's been in a car crash?" said Oz.

"This guy says he's a pro drummer," continued the leader. "Can't wait any longer for Zig."

"Well, he's got the belt, hasn't he?" added one of the group.

Oz looked down at his own belt. He had tried to hide it slightly under his T-shirt and his jeans, but it was very prominent.

"That could catch on, man. We should have got old ones. Where you get it, man?"

"Oh nowhere, it's me grandad's," said Oz. "You won't tell him, will you?"

"Let's give him a chance," said one of the others.

"What's your name anyway?" asked the leader.

"Er, Oz. What's your name, please?"

"I'm Whiz," said the leader. "That's Goz, Daz and Muz. Ziggy's got lost. With your name and your belt, you fit perfectly."

"Heh, you're not the Zeds are you?" said Oz. "Oh no, you're one of my favourite groups . . ."

"Yeh, we're one of our favourite groups as well," said Whiz.

"Wait till I tell our . . . my class I've met the Grateful Zeds, I mean tell the world, the hemisphere . . ."

"Not just *met* them," said Whiz. "You're gonna play with them, man. Get into the limo, baby . . ."

The limousine sped silently through the London streets, at least Oz presumed he was still in London. The inside was so big and spacious, with a television set and a cocktail cabinet and three telephones, that he could hardly see the windows.

29

He tried to look outside, but the glass turned out to be tinted, making the outside world seem in Technicolor.

"Are we going to Hollywood?" said Oz.

"No, Shepherds Bush," said Whiz.

"I knew we must be in the country by now," said Oz. "Can't see many trees, though."

The limousine drew up outside the main gates of the BBC Television Centre. About twenty young girls rushed forward, holding autograph books, and tried to reach the limousine.

Oz was sure he recognized a couple from his class, Tracey and Michelle, but both were wearing Girl Guide uniforms. He decided he must be mistaken, confused by the tinted windows.

The barriers of the main gates went up and the limousine sailed through, leaving the girls behind.

"Here, put these on," said Whiz, throwing Oz some clothes.

They were now in a large dressing room. In a corridor outside were lots of producers and assistants with clip boards, make-up ladies carrying little boxes, and men with earphones and walkie-talkies, all of them bustling about, looking very important.

"Oh, I can't really take this off . . ." said Oz, nervously. Even unbuckling his belt might result in awful consequences.

"Not the belt, man. Keep that on."

Oz did what he was told, carefully not touching his belt, pulling on his stage trousers over his jeans.

When they were all ready, the Zeds went down a long corridor, laughing and talking, pushing and shoving each other, putting on funny voices. At least Whiz, Daz, Goz and Muz were all larking around, having been on television programmes many times before.

Oz, the newest recruit to the Zeds, was becoming slightly worried. In his heart and in his head, he knew he could play the drums, now that he was eighteen, grown up and ever so mature. But doing it for the first time, live on television, with millions watching, that could be a trifle difficult.

"Er, do we get any time to warm up?" asked Oz.

"Whatcha fink this is?" said Daz. "White Hart Lane?"

"We could be there soon," said Whiz. "I've put

in my take-over bid. If Elton John can own a football club, I think we should. But a really good one, of course."

Oz didn't know if this was a joke or not. It was possible, for a terribly famous group like the Zeds, who sold millions of records.

"Four minutes to go, Zeds," said a man with earphones on. "You'll be on next. After Paul."

Oz stood at the back of the studio with his new friends, still worried that he might let them down. He suddenly realized who the singer was, performing on stage. It was Paul McCartney.

Oz immediately forgot his nervousness. He tried to get nearer, to see him closer up.

"Wait till I tell my mum . . ."

Thirty seconds before it was time for the Zeds to appear live, on a very special edition of *Topmost of the Pops*, they were escorted to another stage in the studio which Oz had not noticed before. It was lit up, all ready for them, wired for sound, their instruments laid out.

"Now, which end of these sticks do I use?" said Oz to himself. He sat down and examined his various drums and cymbals and equipment, wondering what went where.

All the cameras now turned on the Zeds and Whiz went straight into their latest single, one which was already climbing up the charts.

"Phew, that's lucky," said Oz. "It's one I know. I'd have been stuck with a brand new one."

He did drop his sticks twice, came in when it was a bass guitar solo, fell over his cymbals, caught his foot in a pedal, but nobody seemed to mind or tell him off. He was off camera at the time and the noise was deafening. All around him, scores of screaming young girls and boys were dancing and waving.

It was time for Oz's solo. He could tell it was because all the cameras were pointing at him. He could see their little red lights on top.

He sat up properly, squared his shoulders as his mother had always told him to, and gave his best moody and mean eighteen-year-old smile.

He paused, then suddenly bashed away at everything in sight, both hands hitting every drum and cymbal, both feet bashing every pedal. Several

33

drums fell over and a cymbal rolled across the floor and into the audience, but all the cameras seemed to be focused mainly on his belt. They appeared more interested in that than his *avant garde* drum technique.

There was a huge roar from everyone when the Zeds finished. Oz felt he'd done quite well, considering. He had got the hang of things eventually. The shouts of appreciation had seemed to be the same, regardless of which end of the drum sticks he used.

About a dozen heavy bouncers rushed to take them off the stage, while other assistants cleared away the instruments for the next number.

The Zeds were escorted through the crowds of screaming girls, down the corridor, to their dressing room.

"Not bad, old Oz," said Whiz. "Groovy smile. Loved the belt."

"Well, I hope I didn't let you down. I think I might have played one or two wrong notes . . ."

"No problem," said Daz. "We do that all the time."

"You looked good," said Muz. "That's what

matters. We could do with some new blood. Some of us are getting a bit ancient, mentioning no names, eh Whiz."

"Well, I am almost thirteen," said Oz. "I mean, very nearly nineteen."

They all smiled and patted Oz on the back.

"Oh no," said Oz. "Is that clock right?"

"Usually is," said Whiz. "Being BBC time. ITV is slower, 'cos they have all the adverts . . ."

"I'll have to go," said Oz. "Thanks for the gag, I mean gig . . ."

"Here, write your number down," said Whiz, passing him a notepad and pen. "We might give you a bell some time."

"I haven't quite got used to the cymbals yet. Not sure if I could manage bells . . ."

The dressing-room door opened and in came Paul McCartney.

Oz already had a notebook and pen in his hand, so he went over, rather shyly. Even at eighteen, you can be shy in the presence of real super stars, so Oz thought. "Er, would you give me your autograph?" said Oz.

"Sure," said Paul.

"It's for me mum, actually."

Paul paused for a moment and Oz thought perhaps he had been rude. He should have said it was for himself.

"That makes a change," said Paul, scribbling a few words in the notebook. "They usually say it's for their children."

"Thanks, Paul," said Oz, tearing out the page in the book.

Oz dashed out of the dressing room, then rushed back again, realizing he was still in the stage clothes. He flung them off, put on his ordinary clothes, and ran out of the dressing room.

"Heh, can I have your autograph?" said Paul McCartney. "For my children . . ."

But Oz had gone.

The train from Euston was very crowded, but Oz eventually managed to find a seat.

Behind him, he could hear some girls giggling, and the very bossy voice of Miss Turkey telling them off. By chance, they were all on the same train home.

He tried to make himself small, just in case she happened to see him, which of course he found very hard, being eighteen and so big and tall.

Miss Turkey was reprimanding Tracey and Michelle for disappearing from their group without telling her. They'd missed a most interesting exhibition at the Science Museum, but at least they'd had the sense to catch the correct train.

After Miss Turkey went back to her own seat, the two girls started telling the others what they'd done. They'd gone to the BBC, so they said, met the members of Zed, and got all their autographs.

"What a lie," said Oz, but not too loudly, just in case they heard him.

"Then we sneaked in and watched the show," said Tracey.

"I suppose that might be true," thought Oz.

"And they were doing it live," said Michelle.

"So what," said Sarah, another girl from the same class. "They just mime to their own records. None of them actually plays their instruments. My dad told me. He's an electrician."

"You don't know anything, Sarah. You're just jealous."

Miss Turkey came back and told them all to keep quiet. They should behave themselves properly when in uniform. They had the honour of the 32nd Troop to consider. Anyone might be listening to them.

"Oh, well," said Oz to himself as he got off the train. "I did play real professional drums. I did appear in a pop group. And was on tele. Let's hope Dez got it on his video."

Oz let himself into his grandfather's flat. His grandfather was still watching television, this time with the sound on. Oz listened in the little hall, then crept into the bedroom. He stood for a few moments inside the wardrobe, with his eyes closed, then he hung up the belt safely, in the correct position, so no one would know he had ever removed it.

He let himself out again and ran all the way home, as quickly as possible, which wasn't very fast. When you have twelve-year-old, weedy, spindly legs, at least the pair which Ossie was currently having to use, they always seem to go far too slowly.

"Where have you been?" said his mother. "I was just getting worried."

"Sorry, Mum," replied Ossie. "The train was late."

"How was it, anyway?"

"Oh, the music was great, really good."

"And how about you?"

"How did you know I played?"

"I mean your lesson. You did have one, didn't you?"

"Oh yeh, I was brilliant. Everyone said. Trific. But I'm exhausted now. Very tiring, when you play live before a big audience."

"You mean Mrs Peabody watched as well?"

"And the rest. Probably about ten million saw me, I mean will see me, when I grow up and become a professional pop musician . . ."

Ossie slumped on the sofa while his mother hung up his coat.

"Well, whatever happened, you do seem to have enjoyed it. I am pleased. Wait a minute. Where's your violin?"

"What?" said Ossie.

"You haven't brought it home. Oswald Osgood, you are just so careless."

"I dunno where it is," said Ossie.

"You'll have left it at Mr Peabody's. I'll ring him now and tell him you'll collect it tomorrow."

"No, no," said Ossie, jumping up. "He's ill, I mean tired out with the trip to London. I wouldn't ring him now . . ."

"Don't be silly . . ."

Ossie managed to grab the phone before his mother could reach it.

"Here, got you a present from London," said Ossie. He gave her a quick hug and pulled out a sheet of crumpled paper from his trouser pocket.

"I've just remembered, I left my violin at Grandad's. I popped in to see him on the way home, that's why I'm late . . ."

His mother had now completely forgotten the missing violin. She was all smiles as she read what was on the piece of paper.

"To Oz's Mum. All the Best—Paul McCartney."

2

Ossie the Champion Miler

There were two lessons Ossie disliked more than any others, Maths and PE. Now and again Maths could be not too bad, and he was able sometimes to get through a whole work card, with a bit of luck, a bit of guessing, and a bit of help from Flossie Teacake, if she was in the mood to give him a bit of help.

"PE is the Pits," said Ossie to his mother as he was getting ready for school. "They should have it banned. Doesn't do you no good. Just wears you out for other lessons. It's cruelty to children."

"Only for those who can't do it," said his mother. "Or who won't *try*. It's just what you need to make you big and strong."

"I'll never be that. My hormones and enzymes and cellars are against it."

Ossie trudged out of his front door and set off for school, pausing at his front gate to decide whether his wrist had suddenly become terribly stiff, too stiff for school work, and whether it might be best to go back to bed and rest it, just for an hour, till after the first lesson, which happened to be Maths.

"No, she won't believe me. She's as cruel as Botty."

At the corner of his street, he began to think that perhaps his asthma was coming on, all of a sudden, which would mean his mother writing a letter to excuse him from PE, which happened to be the second lesson.

"I could do with a note to excuse me from PE for the rest of term. And the rest of my life."

As he turned the corner, he heard someone shouting his name. It was his mother, running after him, waving something.

"Ossie! Stop! You've left your PE things."

Mrs Osgood took Ossie's Spurs bag from his hand and shoved in his school gym shoes, his shorts and PE top.

"If you forgot them deliberately, and made me run after you, I'll be very . . ."

" 'Course I didn't. Just a mistake," said Ossie.

"I am human."

"And you also left this behind, you silly boy," said his mother. "Your towel."

She shoved that in his bag as well, telling him he'd better hurry himself up, or he really would be late.

"Go on, run," she said. "If you can run."

"Horrible," said Ossie, managing a sort of trot for two or three metres, till his mother was out of sight.

"I think I hate PE most of all, even more than Maths. At least with Maths, they don't make you have a shower afterwards . . ."

Mr Bott, head of PE, was demonstrating a new forward roll, which in a moment he wanted all the class to do.

Ossie was hardly listening, as he knew he wouldn't be able to do it. Desmond and Craig would be best. They always were.

"I can't help being so small. Not my fault. I can't even reach the stupid horse, never mind get over it. Who wants to do a bread roll anyway."

Craig and Desmond pushed and shoved to be

first in line to go over, wanting to be the stars. Ossie hung around at the back, managing to let lots of people get ahead of him, so that he could remain at the back of the queue.

"Are you shaking, Ossie Osgood?" said Bonzo, a big fat boy, who was almost as useless at gym as Ossie was, though he did have more of an excuse, being so overweight. "You're scared to go over, aren't you?" said Bonzo.

"Get lost," said Ossie. He hated being stuck with Bonzo, lumped together as two physical failures, the Fatty and the Thinny.

"It's the rotten cold," said Ossie. "They never heat this stupid gym. My legs are frozen. OK for you, with all your layers of fat."

Bonzo gave Ossie a shove, which Ossie didn't mind as it sent him out of the queue and even more people were able to get ahead of him.

"Come out here, boy," shouted Mr Bott. "You, Osgood. I saw you messing about in the line. And I haven't seen you go over yet, have I?"

"You might have missed me," said Ossie. "I do go rather fast."

"Less of the lip, boy," said Mr Bott. "My slipper

44

will go rather fast in a minute. Right, you're next."

All the class stood to one side, waiting to watch Ossie go over the wooden horse, or try to.

In his mind, Ossie felt he could do all the gym work quite easily. He wasn't at all like Bonzo, totally uncoordinated. If only his arms were not so thin, he could climb ropes as well as anyone else. If only his legs were not like match sticks, he would have the strength to jump over real horses, not just wooden ones.

"If only I was eighteen," thought Ossie to himself. "Mum's promised me I'll be really big by then. Some hope."

"Hurry up, boy. Stop day-dreaming. We haven't got all morning."

Ossie walked slowly towards the horse, then stopped, looking at it fearfully as if it might bite him.

"That's not the way," bellowed Mr Bott. "It doesn't matter how small you are, if you approach it in the right manner, determined to get over, anyone can do it. It's like life itself. You have to run for it."

Everyone exchanged looks. One thing they hated more than Mr Bott and his slipper was Mr Bott and his corny sayings.

"Come back here and do it again."

This time Ossie did manage a sort of run, of about ten metres. He was soon wheezing and out of breath, and had slowed right down by the time he reached the horse. He was forced to climb up and on to it. On top, it felt like Everest, with the whole

world below, all watching him. Very slowly, he lowered himself down the other side.

Everyone laughed. Even Bonzo.

In the changing rooms, Desmond and Craig were playing the usual silly games, flicking each other with their towels. Ossie was playing his usual game, keeping well out of the way.

"I want everyone undressed and in that shower in ten seconds," said Mr Bott. "And that includes you, Osgood."

"If Ossie takes his clothes off, sir," said Desmond, "you won't be able to see him."

"Very funny," said Ossie. Desmond was supposed to be his best friend. He'd get him back for that. Some year.

Ossie hated showers. It wasn't just having to display his spindly body to the world, but the act of being wet, having to be immersed in water.

"It's bad for you, too many showers," Ossie muttered to Bonzo. "You lose the body's natural oils. I read that in a magazine."

"I said hurry up," repeated Mr Bott, closing the changing-room door and going into his little office.

47

"Anyway, I had a bath only last week," said Ossie. "No need to have another, not for the rest of the term, the rest of my life."

Ossie let everyone get ahead, then he slowly followed them all into the showers. But he didn't actually go into them.

It was quite remarkable, for someone not apparently gifted as a gymnast, how he managed to weave in and out of the bodies, working his way round the sides, avoiding any stray pools, missing any misdirected jets, so that he had been through the showers—without ever getting wet.

At the end, he came to the sink and quickly turned on both taps. He ducked his head in, for the briefest of seconds, just enough to get the front of his hair and face wet.

Ossie wrapped his towel round himself and was standing there, shivering, when Mr Bott reappeared. "That's more like it. We might make something of you yet, Osgood."

On Friday afternoon, it was Games, which Ossie quite liked, though he wasn't much good, not a star and in all the year teams like Craig and

Desmond. Not yet, anyway.

He consoled himself with the knowledge that in a few years' time, when he was eighteen, he would be in every football team. He had natural talents and consummate skills and probably even an educated left foot. It only needed a bit of muscle, a bit of height, and he'd be there. All the First Division scouts would be knocking at his front door.

"She probably won't let them in. She'll say 'Oswald's doing his music practice.' She'll send them away, not knowing they've come straight from White Hart Lane, just to see me."

Ossie had cleaned his football boots for once. After Games each week, he usually left them around at home, hoping his mother would clean them. He was putting them on when he noticed that no one else had brought their boots with them.

"I dunno, you lot need reminding all the time. I don't know how you manage."

"What you talking about?" said Desmond. "Didn't you see the notice? It's trainers today. Old Botty wants us to practise for the athletics."

"Oh no," said Ossie. "Well, I'm going sick."

"I've got a spare pair I'll lend you," said

Desmond. "As you are my best friend."

On the pitch, Mr Bott was explaining about the County Games being held tomorrow. For their hundredth anniversary, the County Athletics Club were having a big meeting, with international events, as well as races for local schools.

Ossie was more concerned about his feet. They felt funny in someone else's shoes, like trying to put a jelly into the wrong mould, or wearing someone else's face.

"Are you listening, Osgood? We're going to have heats and the best four will run for the school tomorrow."

Mr Bott divided everyone up into heats of ten, but two people were left over, Ossie and Bonzo.

"I've got a special job for you two, though I'm not so sure about you, Osgood."

Mr Bott produced some white finishing tape and measured it out. He told them both where to stand, and then gave one end to Bonzo, and one end to Ossie.

"Now take it carefully, Osgood. I don't want you exhausting yourself. This tape might prove a trifle too heavy for you . . ."

Everyone laughed. Most of all Bonzo.

It was Saturday morning and the High Street was very busy, even busier than normal. Every pavement was crowded and every supermarket was filled with shoppers.

Out of Tesco's came a quarter-filled trolley, closely followed by the quarter-filled figure of Ossie.

"If only I was bigger, I'd do better in the battles. You'd think it was a war. They should give you medals. A VC for every trolley you can fill."

"Where are you going with that trolley, son?" said one of the assistant managers. "They must not leave the shop premises."

"I captured it," said Ossie, "so I thought I'd take it home as a trophy, just as my grandad's got his war souvenirs."

Ossie was made to unload the two carrier bags he had put inside. He then set off slowly towards his grandad's, one bag in each hand, resting every few steps.

Ossie had been so busy moaning and groaning to

himself, convinced his arms were stretching like elastic, that he hadn't noticed Desmond, standing outside a sports shop.

"Hello, Ossie," said Desmond.

"Huh," said Ossie, giving a little grunt. Desmond was quite lucky to get a grunt. Often Ossie said nothing at all to people when he met them, even his best friends.

"I'm waiting for me mum," said Desmond. "See those Nike shoes. I'm getting them. She's promised. They're the very best you can get. They've got spikes, see."

"Whatcha want spikes for? You got a job in the park, picking up litter?"

"For running, stupid. I'm running for the first year this afternoon. I'm in the team. Against schools from everywhere."

"Who wants to go to the stupid old sports?" said Ossie.

"You do," said Desmond. "Sebastian Coe is running in the Invitation Mile."

"My invitation must still be in the post," said Ossie. "Anyway, I don't care. I've got better things to do this afternoon."

"Why, what are you doing?" said Desmond. "Growing?"

"Here's your shopping, Grandad," shouted Ossie, letting himself into the little flat. "I got everything on the list but there was no salt so I asked this horrible manager bloke and he said it was moved to another shelf but I couldn't find it and anyway it was very high up so I didn't know what to do and anyway I was tired and anyway I just got you this instead . . ."

"I don't want the running commentary," said Grandad. "Just the food."

Ossie took a large bottle of HP sauce from one of the bags and handed it to his grandfather who was sitting in front of the TV, about to devour a large bacon sandwich.

"I know you're getting low on HP, so I thought it would be OK . . ."

"I've left you some bacon," said Grandad. "Pull up a sandwich and sit down."

This was one of Grandad's regular jokes, which he made almost every Saturday morning, when Ossie brought the shopping and they had a late breakfast together. Ossie always cut bread so that each slice was like a doorstep.

"God, it was so tiring today."

"Don't say God, your mother wouldn't like it."

"She's not here, or else I couldn't be having this bacon sandwich. Nor this HP. She says it's poison."

"It's lucky I like poison," said Grandad. "I've had it every day for eighty years. Done me no harm."

"I thought you were only sixty-nine, Grandad?"

Ossie put away the shopping. When he returned to the living room, the television commentator was talking about the big County Sports.

"You'll be going along, I suppose," said Grandad. "It says there's races for schoolboys as well."

"Yeh, well, they wanted me to be in the school team, but I said I was too busy, helping me old grandad of eighty . . ."

"Bloomin' heck," said Grandad. "He says they're expecting over ten thousand."

"Don't say bloomin'. Mum doesn't like it."

"No wonder the town was so busy this morning,

if they're expecting all those people."

"How do you know, Grandad? You haven't been out, have you?"

"I have my sources," said Grandad mysteriously.

"You haven't been to the pub, have you?"

"I told you, I have my sources. OK sauce, Daddie's sauce. And now HP sauce . . ."

Grandad laughed so much at his own joke that he started choking on his sandwich.

Ossie waited till he had recovered, then said he had to go. Ossie opened the front door, then closed it loudly. He stopped and waited. Grandad had obviously settled down in front of the television again.

Ossie crept back down the little hall and slowly opened Grandad's bedroom door.

He clambered over all the boxes and piles and reached the wardrobe. The belt was inside, exactly as he'd left it. He put it on carefully, closed his eyes, and wished very hard that once again he could be eighteen.

"Oh, I've just got to be big and strong and most

of all fast. And I want to be it now. At once."

When he opened his eyes, the belt fitted perfectly.

Looking in the mirror, he could see a tall, eighteen-year-old youth staring straight back at him, a very fit, very athletic-looking Oz.

Over the tannoy came an announcement about the Invitation Mile. Three of the greatest milers in the world were gracing the sports with their presence, but as this was a gala, a special day in the history of the Club, it had been decided to include one representative of local talent.

Oz was standing in the middle of the densest part of the crowd, but managing to get a very good view. When you're eighteen and tall and well built, there is no difficulty in seeing over people's heads.

He was hardly listening to the announcement over the tannoy, as he was watching the Under 13 Boys race, which was taking place in a corner of the stadium.

"Look at poor old Desmond," said Oz. "He hasn't got a chance. Oh no, he's hobbling already. Imagine wearing new shoes for a big race. He's had to pack up. Perhaps I'd better go and carry him."

The tannoy came on again, saying that an eliminating heat for the Mile would start in five minutes.

"And anyone can enter, just as long as they live in the County and are over eighteen years of age. Thank you, ladies and gentlemen."

Almost fifty people were getting ready for the start, most of them in proper running clothes, with spikes and tops which boasted the names of their local schools and clubs.

They had obviously known in advance that there was going to be an all-comers heat.

There was one very tough-looking, immaculately track-suited figure doing warm-up exercises, running on the spot, punching the air, bending and twisting, showing off his muscles. He pulled off his track suit to reveal a light blue running vest which said "Cambridge University" on the front.

"I didn't know *he* went here," said Oz to himself. "I bet he just bought it in a street market."

Oz was still standing in the crowd, undecided

whether he should take part, as he didn't have proper clothes. But the sight of Mr Bott, displaying his flash exercises and his Cambridge colours, made Oz think he might just have a go. He vaulted the crowd barrier with one leap.

"Jolly good, jolly good," said a marshal in a red blazer, going round all the runners. "Jolly good turn out. It is meant to be a bit of a fun run, this heat. The serious race will be later. Right, could you now all get in line!"

"I say you," said Mr Bott, turning to Oz, presuming that a youth in jeans could not possibly be in the race. "Would you go and get me some blocks?"

"Blocks?" said Oz, not understanding. "Building blocks to play with? Or do you mean ice-cream blocks to cool you down? Give us the money then . . ."

"What are you talking about?" said Mr Bott. "Oh, never mind, I'll use them for the real race later, when I've won this one. Just keep out of my way."

There were so many runners that the starting

line was very packed, so the marshal simply held up a flag, said, "Ready, Steady, Go," and off they all went.

Mr Bott was in the lead from the very beginning, possibly because he had moved marginally before anyone else, but the marshal didn't bring them back. It was supposed to be a fun race.

The crowd were cheering at the sight of so many runners in one race, some quite old, well over thirty, while others were more about the same age as Oz. Quite a few pupils were shouting "Come on Botty", pupils of Brookfield Comprehensive who had immediately recognized their PE master.

It was going to be only a two-lap race, not a full mile, to sort out the no-hopers. Oz was amongst a group near the back, rather distracted by the crowd shouting, and all the runners pushing and jostling each other. His tummy felt a bit funny as well.

"Perhaps I shouldn't have had that bacon sandwich," he said to himself. "Or poured all that HP sauce on."

But the more he ran, the easier it felt. His legs seemed to move along the track effortlessly. He had no trouble with his breathing at all.

"Heh, no asthma. I knew at eighteen it would go. Mum was right."

Very soon, Oz moved up to half way, without really trying. At the end of the first lap, he was in the first ten. As they approached the final lap, there were only two runners in it, Oz and Mr Bott. They had even managed to lap several of the other runners.

Oz's feet began to feel a little uncomfortable. He was wearing old jeans, like any other eighteen-year-old, and rather scuffed-up old training shoes. With the bell sounding in his ears, he decided to kick off his trainers and run in his bare feet. The crowd gave a huge cheer. They were now all shouting for him.

Oz got faster and faster, hitting the finishing tape almost twenty metres ahead of the puffing, panting Mr Bott. It had all been so easy. But then when you're eighteen, and a natural athlete, tall and slim, with no worries about your weight, or breathing, you do have an advantage over a much older schoolteacher.

"Thanks for the race," said Oz, hardly out of breath, offering his hand as Mr Bott eventually staggered over the line. Mr Bott was unable to manage anything in reply. He collapsed in a heap on the track.

As he did so, Oz noticed that the tab on the back of his running shirt clearly said "British Home Stores".

The Invitation Mile was the last event of the day. Before it started, the three guest runners kindly agreed to parade round the circuit, sign autographs and present the prizes for the schools races. Steve Ovett waved at everyone. Steve Cram smiled. Sebastian Coe made a little speech, saying how pleased they all were to help the fund-raising and join in the celebrations for the County Sports hundredth anniversary. It was meant to be a fun afternoon, though you never knew, someone could break a world record. There was a big cheer at this.

The announcer said how marvellous it was that three such world-famous runners should give up time for their sports, and let a local runner compete with them—eighteen-year-old Oz Goodbody. That got the biggest cheer of the afternoon so far. Oz didn't mind they'd got his name wrong.

He was in proper running shorts this time, and a top which said "Brookfield School". Mr Bott, having got over his own disappointment, had decided Oz must be an old boy of the school. He was sure he recognized him and insisted he wore real athletic shorts and vest. But Oz said he still wanted to run in bare feet.

"I saw what happened to Dez," Oz explained. "I'm not putting those stupid things on my feet. If Zola Budd can do it, so can I."

"Then what about your belt?" said Mr Bott. "Let me hold it for you. Here, I'll take it off . . ."

"No, no, I'll be lost, I mean last, if I don't wear it . . ."

The marshal used a proper starting pistol for the Invitation Mile, which rather alarmed Oz. He immediately put his hands to his ears, which meant he set off behind the other three.

But he soon caught them up, or perhaps it was because the others slowed down. They were either taking their time, being terribly experienced mile-runners, or perhaps for this gala event they wanted to give the local boy a little bit of a chance, at least in the early stages.

For the first lap, the four kept up the same pace, neck by neck. It was a great help to Oz, running against such seasoned runners. They set the pace and encouraged him, telling him how well he was doing.

By the time they came to the second lap, Oz

63

could sense they were starting to move a little bit faster, trying perhaps to throw him off, or perhaps throw off each other. But Oz found that as they ran faster, he could run faster as well.

Suddenly, on the third lap, Steve Ovett made a break and sprinted ahead of the other four.

"I've seen this happen on TV," thought Oz. "He's the pace-maker. He steps up the pace for a while, then someone else does it. That's how they get world records. I'll just keep tucked in behind."

Oz was looking at Coe and Cram, wondering who would be next, when he realized they had just passed Steve Ovett—standing at the side of the track. He was clutching his stomach and appeared to be in agony, making very strange faces.

"Oh, poor Steve," thought Oz. "I get those pains sometimes, when I've eaten too quickly, especially apples."

Steve Cram then took the lead, but as the bell went for the last lap, he stopped running and started hobbling on one leg.

"I've pulled," muttered Cram, waving Oz on. "It's up to you, now, Oz."

"What did he say?" Oz asked Sebastian Coe, as

64

they ran side by side, step for step. "What has he pulled? I didn't see him pull anything."

"Sorry," said Coe, looking puzzled.

"Oh, I suppose he must have cramp," said Oz. "Cram has got cramp. That's funny, eh?"

Oz started laughing at his own joke. It meant he dropped a few paces behind, forgetting for a moment that he was running in what might prove to be a world-record race, with three of the greatest mile runners.

"Well, one of the greatest. Pity about Ovett and Cram."

Oz sprinted to catch up, which he found surprisingly easy. In fact, he hardly felt out of puff at all. It had all been so interesting that his mind had not dwelt on his wheezing, or his thin legs, or his weak chest, which used to happen, many years ago.

He drew level with Coe on the bend coming into the final straight. He was going so quickly it was as if he was flying, his feet scarcely hitting the track at all.

As he caught up with Coe on the outside, Oz sensed a slight coldness on his left foot as he gently grazed the back of Coe's running shoe.

"Sorry Seb," said Oz, turning round to apologize. "Hope that didn't tickle . . ."

Coe was on the ground. The crowd had risen to its feet and everyone was roaring. One half was shouting, "He's been tripped!" and the other shouting, "Come on, Oz! Come on, Brookfield!"

"No use stopping now," thought Oz. "Mustn't let the crowd down."

Oz finished at such speed that he couldn't stop. He went whizzing once again round the track, before eventually he slowed down.

"That was sensational," said a marshal, all excited. "It could be three fifty."

"Goodness, is it that late?" said Oz. "My tea will be ready soon."

"It really could be a three-fifty mile! The first in the history of the world."

"We'll have to wait for official ratification," said another official. "So I'm not sure if it will count."

"You mean because of my bare feet," said Oz. "Or because I'm too little, I mean too young. I am only eighteen."

"There was an enormously high wind today," said the marshal. "Anyway let me take you to the

66

dressing room. I'm sure you'll want a shower."

"A shower!" said Oz. "You must be joking."

With that, Oz jumped over a rail into the crowd and disappeared.

Ossie closed the door of his grandfather's bedroom. He had put the belt back safely, closed his eyes, wished, and was once again his twelve-year-old self.

"Hello, Grandad," he said, opening the living-room door.

"You gave me a fright. Didn't hear you come in."

Grandad had been snoozing in front of the TV, which was flickering away, the sound off.

"Did you go to the sports then?" said Grandad.

"I saw a bit of it," replied Ossie.

"So did I," said Grandad. "But I switched off when that clown pulled a muscle. I knew what was coming. Seen it all before. They can't fool me. Huh, these so-called Invitation Miles."

"I'm sure you're right," said Ossie. "You haven't got a plaster, have you? I think I've got a little cut on the big toe of my left foot. It's as if it's been spiked . . ."

3

Ossie and the Squat

"There are going to be some changes around here," said Ossie's mother. "Are you listening, Oswald Osgood?"

"Can't avoid it, with you shouting," said Ossie. He had Dez's Walkman on, so he couldn't hear his mother's words, but he knew she was shouting something. He could tell from her face, and the way her lips moved.

"Take that thing off when I'm talking to you," she said.

"All right, all right, keep your hair on, wigs are dear," said Ossie. That was one of his grandad's phrases.

"From now on, there are going to be new rules in this place."

"I thought this was a house," said Ossie, slowly taking off his headphones. "Not a prison."

"You'll go too far one of the days, my lad, with all of your cheek."

"Look, can't you see I'm busy, woman."

Ossie was sitting at the living-room table, surrounded by his comics, his tapes, his best felt pens, notepads, football books, football photographs, old Spurs programmes, quiz books and other essentials of life. The TV was on, as Lucy and Mrs Osgood were waiting for a nature programme, and so was Ossie, when he wasn't concentrating on the Walkman, his comics or his football books.

"I thought you were supposed to be doing your homework," said his mother.

"What do you think I'm doing?" said Ossie, trying quickly to find his Maths book which he was sure he had somewhere on the table.

"You've been sitting there an hour and you haven't even opened it yet."

"Look, don't shout at me. My ears are sore."

"Well, you shouldn't put that stupid Walkman on."

"It's all your fault," said Ossie. "You made me."

"What *are* you talking about? How do I make

you? Come on, explain."

Ossie muttered and mumbled, sighing and groaning as he made a big show of looking for his Maths book. It was still in his sports bag. He hadn't taken it out yet.

"If you weren't so rotten to me," said Ossie, "and such selfish pigs, I could play my tapes properly, like normal people, 'stead of having to borrow a Walkman. Oh yes, everyone else can do that, but *you two*, huh huh, I'm not allowed to make any noise in this house, surprised I'm allowed to breathe, just 'cos *you two* are watching some soppy nature programme, think you're the bosses of the whole world . . ."

Mrs Osgood suddenly jumped up and grabbed Ossie by the arm, forcing his face round so he had to pay attention to what she was saying.

"You have your own room! There is no need at all for you to be in here when you're doing your homework. Why do you have to distract everyone else with your noise and your mess? Answer me that."

"But I'm not doing my homework," said Ossie, sullenly.

"That's precisely the point!" said his mother. "You *should* be. Look at the time. I want you in bed in half an hour, so you'd better go up and do your homework, *now*."

"Please keep quiet, Ossie," said Lucy, ever so charmingly. "I'm trying to listen. Miss said we had to watch this programme and she's going to ask us questions tomorrow because it's terribly useful, isn't it, Mum?"

Ossie got up very wearily and started to clear his things away. He liked being in the living room. He liked being with his own family. It wasn't just that he feared he might miss something, by being upstairs. He enjoyed the warmth and company of Lucy and his mother.

"Most of the world have *not* got a room of their own," said his mother. "I never had my own room at your age. You're a very lucky boy."

"Oh, not that one again."

He gathered up his stuff, shoving things any old how into his Spurs bag.

"Don't do that with your Maths book! No wonder you lose marks for untidyness."

"Oh, well, if nobody wants me. Not much point in being here. Not much point in being anywhere. Not much point in living, seems to me . . ."

"Oh, stop moaning and being sanctimonious. It doesn't suit you."

"I think I'll probably emigrate. If I'm not here tomorrow morning, I'll be on my way to Australia, then you'll be sorry, then you'll regret being horrible to me."

"Shut up, will you. The programme's starting."

"Sorry I spoke," said Ossie.

"And when you get to your room, I want it all cleared up, all that rubbish chucked out and everything put in the drawers or on your shelves, and if you don't hang those clothes up once and for all, they've been lying there for three weeks and I'm certainly not going to . . ."

"Rabbit rabbit rabbit," said Ossie.

There was a glint in his mother's eye. Ossie saw it just in time and made a quick dash for the door, getting out before she could catch him. He could hear her closing the door firmly behind him. Keeping him out.

" 'Snot fair," said Ossie, slowly trudging up the stairs.

From below, he thought he could hear Lucy and his mother giggling.

"Wonder what they've got to laugh at. Can't be that stupid nature programme. That's always really boring. Just like those two. Just like this whole boring house . . ."

At school next day, Dez whispered in the middle of Maths that he had something important to say to Ossie. But he couldn't tell him till later.

At lunchtime, in the playground, Dez insisted he had to be captain and he would pick both sides. If his team won, he would be able to tell Ossie whatever it was he was going to tell him, depending on how the game went, depending on how many goals he, Desmond, scored.

Desmond's team did win, and he scored four goals, but then Desmond was a fouler when it came to playground football, so Ossie maintained. He pushed people around, just because he was big and fat, especially littler and thinner people, such as Ossie.

Before the end of school, said Desmond, he'd let Ossie know. Perhaps.

"What a big head," thought Ossie. "He thinks

he's it. I hate people like that. People who are having parties and you have to go creep creep to them for days, just so's they'll invite you. Or they tell you their dad is taking them to a match and they can take one friend, so you have to be all nice to them for yonkers and yonkers. Makes me sick. I hate that Desmond. Wish he wasn't my best friend."

All the same, Ossie was intrigued. Could it be a party? No, Desmond had his birthday months ago. Was there a good match tomorrow?

All afternoon, Ossie wondered what it could be.

The only bright spot in the day was the last lesson, the last before the weekend, which was History.

Miss Turkey was in a good mood, for once, and she chose Ossie to take a note to the school secretary.

Ossie wasn't sure whether this counted as a big compliment or not. It could mean she considered you still a baby, to be impressed by such things. Flossie Teacake had jumped up and said, "Me, Miss, me, Miss," the moment Miss Turkey called for volunteers. Desmond had also looked expectant. So Ossie was rather pleased to be chosen.

He took the long way round. In such a big school, most of the ways were long, but Ossie chose the long scenic route, through the gym, round the swimming pool, in between the art rooms, past the metalwork shops, into the media resources room, into the girls' lavatory only to say sorry and come out, then into the television studio, a real one, where the school made their own little video films, but for sixth formers only, which Ossie thought was most unfair.

"Not a bad school, really," thought Ossie to himself. "There's always lots to do and see. If only we hadn't got lessons. That's what spoils it all. It would be mass doss, just walking round all day."

"Mass doss" was the latest slang. He'd heard older boys using it, but he wasn't quite sure what it meant.

As he was coming back from the secretary's office, Ossie noticed that the door of the sixth-form common room was open. No first year was ever allowed inside. In fact you could get thumped for just going past the door.

There were only two people inside, as far as he could see, a boy with very long hair and ear-rings, and a punky girl lying on a couch. Neither was looking his way. Both were slumped deep in their seats, slurping coffee.

"So you going tomorrow then?" said the boy.

"Where's it at then?" asked the girl.

"The new squat. You know. In Southfields, number eleven. Everybody's going. Be well smart."

"Probably," said the girl. "My mum's chucked me out, so I'll have to end up somewhere."

"They've got electricity, gas, everyfink," said the boy. "Brilliant. Best squat I've ever been in."

"You staying there then?"

" 'Course. Got so many bedrooms you wouldn't believe it."

"Sounds well swift," said the girl.

Ossie's little ears were pricked up. He'd just got to grips with the expression "mass doss", or so he thought, but now the new phrase appeared to be "well smart" and "well swift", whatever that meant.

"Here, what's that kid doing?"

The girl suddenly rolled off the couch, on to the floor, laughing and giggling. She had just noticed Ossie, his little nose peeking through the crack in the door, listening to every word.

"I'll have you," shouted the boy, looking very angry, pretending to jump up and chase Ossie.

Ossie was off, racing down the corridor, back to his classroom. The fast way, not the scenic way.

Ossie and Desmond were walking part of the way home together, which they often did, if they were speaking to each other.

"Glad it's Friday," said Desmond. "Fed up with that rotten school."

"What you doing tomorrow, Dez?" asked Ossie.

"Lots of things."

"Is your dad taking you to Arsenal?" asked Ossie.

"Who? Load of rubbish. Gone off them. I support Man U now."

Ossie could never understand people who changed their allegiances. He would support Spurs even if they were in the fourth division, so he always told people.

"I might go to Watford," said Dez, "on me own."

"She wouldn't let you," said Ossie.

"Who?"

"Your old woman."

"She wouldn't know."

"I might go to Luton," said Ossie. "On me own. On the train."

"She wouldn't let you," said Desmond.

"Who?"

"That old biddy that lives in your house, wassername."

Ossie swung his sports bag at Desmond, catching him on the back of the legs. Desmond did the same. They stood on the crowded pavement, swinging at each other, pretending to be really angry, as shoppers tried to get past, till at last they both collapsed exhausted in the gutter, laughing at each other and themselves.

"Look at your trousers," said Desmond. "Filthy. You'll be for it."

"Well, what about your bag," said Ossie. "The handle's bust and there's holes in it."

"That's how I like it. Seen that new kid in our class with his new bag and his new school shoes? What a wally."

"Yeh, I don't like having new things or clean things," said Ossie. "If I just left these trousers like this, then it wouldn't matter getting them dirty, 'cos they'd already be dirty. Stands to reason."

"See you, Ossie."

"See you, Dez."

They'd now come to the parting of the ways. Desmond was cutting across the park, to get to his home.

"Oh, Ossie," he shouted. "Forgot to tell you. You can come to my house tomorrow night. Stay the night and everyfink. I gotta new computer game, a football one, really good. Come about six, eh? All right?"

Ossie thought for a moment. Desmond could be a pain sometimes, but a night out was a night out. Better than staying at home and being moaned at all weekend.

"Yeh. Fanks. See yer, Dez."

"See yer, Ossie."

It was Saturday evening, just before five o'clock, and Ossie was about to leave his front door. He was carrying his pyjamas, his toothbrush, his hair-brush, his sponge bag, his asthma inhaler, just in case he got over-excited and started wheezing, clean underpants for the next day, a clean T-shirt for the next day, an extra pullover, slippers for night-time, wellies in case it rained, a raincoat in case it rained, fifty pence in case they went anywhere and Ossie would have to pay his way, and a bunch of flowers and leaves, freshly picked from the back garden, a present for Mrs Peacock for having Oswald for the night.

It was all utterly pointless, so Ossie thought, cluttering him up with all that stuff. But having to carry a bunch of flowers, through the street, in full public view, *that* was the stupidest thing of all.

"I'm just going to dump these lousy twigs in the first dustbin," said Ossie, shouting back through his letterbox. Lucy was at the front window, waving to him, rather sad that he was going away for the night. She would have no one to play with, and no one to argue with.

The door suddenly opened and his mother rushed out. Ossie thought at first he was going to be for it, because he'd shouted at her through the letterbox.

"Forgotten this," she said. "You might need it."

She shoved something into Ossie's sports bag, gave him a quick kiss and a hug, then went back inside and closed the front door, joining Lucy at the window to wave after him as he set off.

The minute he got to the front gate, Ossie put his hand in his sports bag to see what stupid thing she'd now given him. It turned out to be his teddy bear.

He had had it for years, since he was about three. It had only one leg and a chewed-up ear. Ossie himself had chewed it, getting to sleep at night. At one time, he had refused to go to bed without his teddy.

"What do I want this for?" he moaned. "I haven't used this, oh I dunno, for days and days. She thinks I'm still a baby, that old bat. Always bossing me around."

Through the window, it looked as if Lucy and his mother were laughing.

Ossie and his grandad were listening to *Sports Report* together on the radio.

Each of them loved doing this, though they would never have admitted it. It meant Ossie could drone on, analysing every result, every goal scorer, how far up or down the League Spurs now were, how lucky Arsenal had been, without either his mother or Lucy telling him to keep quiet.

As for Grandad, he got Ossie to fill in all the scores in his *Daily Express*. His eyes were not up to it these days, nor his ears. He needed to get the scores all down correctly and as quickly as possible, as he might have to ring up Littlewoods straight away and claim his two and a half million pounds.

ANONYMOUS WAR HERO WINS BIGGEST EVER FOOTBALL POOLS.

Every Saturday evening, as five o'clock approached, both Ossie and Grandad could see in their minds the headlines.

I OWE IT ALL TO MY GRANDSON. I WILL SEE HIM ALL RIGHT.

But, as ever, at seven minutes past five o'clock on Saturday evening, Grandad was cursing and swearing, tearing up his football coupon, saying he was never going to waste his money, ever again.

"What would you do if you did win, Grandad?" said Ossie.

"Get out of this place, pretty damn quick."

"So would I," said Oz. "I'd live on my own in a huge house with millions of rooms and every time one room got filled up with stuff I'd move into the next one. I'd never clean anything, ever again."

"Is that all?" said Grandad.

"Then I'd buy a sweet shop."

Grandad laughed. Then he got up and switched on the television.

"Cup of tea, Grandad?" said Ossie.

"You've taken your time," said Grandad.

Ossie went to the little kitchen alcove and put on the kettle. At the same time, he picked up Grandad's phone. With the kettle starting to boil, and the noise of the TV, he knew Grandad would never hear him.

"That you, Dez," said Ossie on the phone. "Yeh, load of wallies. Don't go on about it. Spurs will still win the League. Anyways, just wanna say I can't come. Me mum says I can't. Got to stay at home. Sorry about that. Yeh, stupid old bat. See yer, Dez."

Ossie gave his grandfather his tea, remembering to put in two sugars for him, then he said he would have to go now.

Instead of leaving the flat, he went into the

bedroom, put down his sports bag, opened the wardrobe and thought long and hard.

"Desmond's mum is worse than my mum. I'd forgotten about her. Why do I want to go there? Just to get bossed around, clean me hands, say please and thank you. I must be mad. If only I was eighteen, this very minute, I could do what I wanted, go anywhere, sleep anywhere, not be told to do this and do that all the time. Oh, if only . . ."

Ossie closed his eyes. When he opened them, he was once again Oz, a very mature sixth former, aged eighteen. He even had an ear-ring. He looked well smart.

Oz found Southfields straight away. It was a broad road, with lots of trees and big houses, a road he knew very well. He'd always imagined it must be full of posh people, like doctors and lawyers and head waiters.

He couldn't believe one of the houses could possibly have become a squat. They all looked so well painted and well cared for.

He walked up and down the road twice, before eventually he worked out which was number

eleven. It didn't have a number, that was the problem. At first sight, it seemed like every other
house, except the front hedge and garden were
rather overgrown.

He went up the driveway and found that the
front door was barricaded. Wooden planks had
been nailed against it and two huge padlocks fitted.
The windows were the same, all boarded up.

"I must be too late," thought Oz. "They've
been chucked out."

He knocked at the door, which was quite difficult, even with his strong, eighteen-year-old
hands, because the boards were so thick and
rough. There was no reply.

Oz noticed a big tree in the front garden, so he
bounded up it, climbing very quickly and easily.
When you're eighteen, trees are very easy to climb.

He could hear music from an upper room, which
made him realize the house was inhabited after all.
He crawled along a branch till he was almost in line
with the window.

"You're not the Old Bill, are you?" said a boy's
voice through a broken window pane.

"Don't be stupid," said a girl's voice. "The Old

Bill can't climb trees. Their feet are too big."

There was a lot of laughter from inside the room and the first boy disappeared. Oz could hear him crashing on the bare floor.

"I'm Oz," said Oz in a loud whisper. "Not Bill. Let me in."

Oz crawled nearer and nearer, but just as he was about to touch the window, the branch began to sag. With a tremendous creaking and crackling, it started splitting from the tree, sending Oz towards the ground.

"Tar—zan," shouted Oz, going with the falling branch. But he timed his fall exactly, bouncing like a rubber ball the moment the branch hit the ground.

He jumped up, beating his chest, giving more Tarzan-like yells.

"When you're eighteen, you're so strong, so big, so fit, so everything . . ."

Several faces had appeared at the upstairs windows, watching Oz jump around. One of them lowered something on a string which hit the top of his head.

Oz fell to the ground, pretending to be unconscious, lying there motionless. The faces at the window looked concerned for a moment.

Then Oz jumped up again, feeling his head, as if examining where he had been injured. At his feet, he found a key. It had been tied to the end of the string. A label on it was marked "Back Door".

"Thanks, mate," said Oz. "Cheers. That was well swift."

He quickly went round to the back of the house and let himself in.

Inside, the house was full of people, all over the place. Many of them were asleep on the floors, wrapped in blankets, but others were busy, doing lots of different things.

Oz went into a large bedroom which had been turned into a motorbike workshop, with bits all over the floor, wheels hanging on the walls, grease and oil everywhere, just like a real garage, only messier.

"This is what houses should be like," said Oz to himself. "I can't even bring my bike into our kitchen to mend a puncture, or she moans at me."

★

He went into another bedroom which had become a recording studio, or so it appeared. There were lots of lights and amplifiers and electric cables. A little stage had been made out of wooden boxes and two boys were arranging some drums.

The boys started beating them, testing them out, turning up the volume, getting louder and louder.

"Nobody tells them to stop," said Oz. "Nobody says put headphones on. This is how all houses should be."

He came next to a kitchen, at least a room which had become a kitchen, with open packets of bread and biscuits scattered everywhere, wholemeal flour, vegetables and lentils, packets of seeds and spices and herbs. He noticed some tins which had been opened, still with food in them. He dipped his finger in a half-full tin of beans and shoved some straight into his mouth.

"Who needs knives and forks," said Oz. "Who needs plates. This is the way to live. I'll come back here later, when I'm hungry."

★

The attic rooms had become workshops, with people making paper flowers, breaking up furniture, painting notices, making kites, cutting up old clothes and dyeing them different colours.

There seemed to be paint everywhere, spattered on the walls and floors.

"Nobody tells them to clear up their mess," said Oz.

A girl who was trying out a new shade of red paint, testing it on the walls, decided to try it on the door as well, just as Oz was standing there, looking in. It went right across his face, but the girl never noticed, nor did Oz say anything.

"I bet you don't have to wash your hands or your face before meals," said Oz. "Not in this place. This is the way everyone should live."

Oz went back down the stairs, or what was left of the stairs. Many of the banisters had gone and several steps were missing.

When he reached the ground floor, he could hear loud shouting and cheering. It came from what must have been the main living room of the house, judging by the size of its doorway. It sounded very much as if it now contained a football pitch. In a *house*?

Oz opened a door and saw about ten boys, most of them sixth formers from his school. They were playing a five-a-side, indoor match, with a real football, with goals marked up on the walls at either end. All the windows were of course boarded up, which was a great help. The ball just bounced back into play.

"Fantastic," said Oz. "I always wanted to play indoor football. I only have to bounce a titchy plastic ball in our front hall, and my mum goes spare."

"You got that key?" shouted a voice from the far end. It was the sixth former with the long hair, the one who had been in the school common room.

Oz tried to hide at first, worried that he might be spotted, told off for trespassing, for listening in to what sixth formers had been saying. Then he realized he was eighteen, one of them, with every right to be here and do what he liked.

"Oh, yeh," said Oz, taking the key from his pocket. He handed it over, still on the long string. "Thanks. Well good of you."

"Right, you can go on their side. You're losing, twenty-three to nine."

Oz scored almost at once, and kept on scoring. Now that he was eighteen, all his talents and skills, hidden for so long inside a rather weedy twelve-year-old frame, emerged for all to see.

When the score got to twenty-three to twenty-two, the other team started complaining, saying Oz was too good.

"He's ruined the game," said one boy. "We've got too many playing now on a pitch this size."

"No problem," said another.

He put his head down, made broom broom noises with his mouth, pretending to kick on the floor as if he was starting a motorbike, then he charged forward at great speed, going straight for the far wall.

Oz stared in amazement. Everyone else cheered. The boy disappeared into the wall and went right through it, leaving a trail of plaster and wallpaper behind.

The wall had already been vandalized, so Oz noticed, with gaps and holes everywhere. It was

only a simple partition anyway, very easy to knock down. Which is what all the other boys started to do, shouting and yelling, kicking and bashing away, till the whole wall was completely demolished.

Then they got a brush and swept all the mess into the corridor, just leaving it there.

The football pitch was now another fifteen metres longer, a perfect size for a game.

"Who needs builders," said Oz. "All houses should be like this. Everybody can build their own extension, if they want to."

★

93

"I like your blusher," said a girl, taking Oz by the hand. "I do like guys who wear make-up. Is it Mary Quant or Elizabeth Arden?"

"Dulux, I think," said Oz, feeling his face, having forgotten he'd been painted by mistake.

The football game had given way to a party. It just seemed to happen. The minute the match was over, people started bringing in instruments, guitars and drums, and rigging up lights.

"Are you gonna dance or what?" said the girl. She had on a miniskirt, fishnet stockings and pink hair which stuck up in the air like a peacock's.

Oz wasn't sure what you did, when you did dancing, though he'd seen them doing it at first hand on *Topmost of the Pops*.

The girl stood about a metre away from Oz and swayed back and forward, her eyes closed, her feet in the same position all the time, clicking her fingers.

Oz did the same. He found it really very easy.

"Do you come here often?" said the girl.

"Well, usually my mum won't let me out in the evenings, not after six," said Oz. The girl laughed.

"I haven't been home after six for weeks," said

the girl. "Fact is, I haven't been home. Full stop."

So Oz stopped. She grabbed him by the hand and told him to start grooving again.

They drifted towards the guitars and drums, but Oz had to put his hands over his ears. Then he remembered. At eighteen, you love really loud music. Everyone knows that.

"Do you like punch?"

"I don't know," said Oz. "I've never read it, but my mum always reads it when she goes to the dentist's."

"I mean the drink, dum dum. Try it. It's great."

Oz tried a few sips. There were great chunks of fruit and vegetables in it, plus leaves and twigs.

The girl finished hers in one gulp and asked Oz to go and get her some more, pointing to a corner.

He went across and found a huge, cracked, old-fashioned washing-up bowl, with a great pile of decaying fruit and vegetables floating on top of what looked like dirty washing-up water. He felt sick at the sight of it.

"If Mum knew I'd been drinking from that!" said Oz. "Ugh."

★

Oz suddenly felt very tired. All the noise and crowds had made his ears and head ache. There were so many people smoking that he was beginning to choke. He was worried that he might start to wheeze, which of course was unthinkable.

All the same, he was finding breathing a bit difficult. Then there was his stomach. Even those few sips of that disgusting stuff had made him feel funny.

"I'm well knackered," he said to the girl. "I gotta go."

He was worried that the girl would ask him where he was going, but she just nodded, accepting it.

"That's one thing about being eighteen," thought Oz. "People don't ask you who you are, what you do, where you're from, where you're going."

He paused and thought. "I wonder where I *am* going?"

Oz had fallen asleep on an old bed in one of the attics.

It had felt good at first, just falling in a heap

when he was tired, not bothering to get washed, or clean his teeth, or even take his clothes off, and of course there was nobody around to tell him off.

But he did feel a bit cold, and rather itchy. He scratched his back, and his leg, then his arms. Then he decided it was his hair that was itching most of all.

"Oh, no, don't say I've got fleas."

He jumped up and shook his blankets, the ones he had thrown over himself. They turned out to be old carpets and rags.

He began to cough. It might have been the dust, or perhaps a cold coming on.

He tried to lie down again and find a comfortable position, hoping to get back to sleep, but someone had started on the drums downstairs, banging and banging, turning up the volume. He could hear lots of other shouts and crashes from different parts of the house.

"Oh, no, I'll never get back to sleep again."

After a while he got up, looking for the bathroom to have a drink of water.

The bathroom, when he found it, was full of

broken bits of a Mini car which someone had started to put together, then abandoned. Oz turned on a tap, but nothing happened, except the whole house shook.

He found a lavatory, pushed open the door with a struggle, and jumped back in alarm. A skeleton was hanging from the ceiling, its feet in the water. All over the floor were skulls and sheep's heads. The smell was terrible.

He tried once more to get back to sleep, but without any luck. Several people fell over him, looking for the bathroom. In the end, when dawn had at last started to arrive, he decided he would get up.

"Haven't slept, anyway. Might as well just have some breakfast and go home."

Oz staggered downstairs, trying to avoid all the other sleeping bodies, and headed for the kitchen.

He picked up a packet of bread and was just about to eat a slice, when he realized it was covered in mould.

"Ugh, that was lucky."

He decided to try a cupboard, just in case there

were any unopened tins of beans left by the previous occupants, the sort of stores for emergencies his mother always kept. Then he let out a terrifying yell.

Oz's screams were so loud that people started running down the stairs, asking if there was a fight, was someone being murdered, had the pigs sent Alsatians, had there been an explosion, were they being raided?

"Watch out!" cried Oz, as he ran across the kitchen as fast as he could, colliding with people coming to see what all the commotion was about.

Out of the cupboard had come a whole family of rats, huge fat ones, furious at being disturbed when they were working their way round all the rotting food. The biggest had thrown itself straight at Oz's hand.

Oz ran all round the ground floor at great speed, chased by the giant rat. There was no way out, as all the windows and doors were boarded up, which Oz had forgotten.

At even greater speed, he raced upstairs to the first floor, found the broken window, and with a huge leap he managed to grab a strong branch of

99

the tree and swing himself to the ground.

He ran along the road to his grandad's, as fast as his rather tired, rather worn, rather dirty, rather itchy eighteen-year-old body could take him.

"Goodness, you're hungry," said his mother. "Didn't they feed you at Desmond's house?"

"Well, I didn't want to eat too much. You know what it's like. Don't wanna seem greedy. That's what you've always told me, Mum."

"How considerate of you."

"Anyway, the food wasn't as good as yours, Mum," said Ossie.

"What are *you* after? I don't usually get compliments at this time of the morning."

"It was rotten, really, the food, you should have seen the mould."

"Mould? I can't believe it. I'm told Mrs Peacock is far more houseproud than I am."

"I mean mouldy portions, titchy helpings, that's what I mean."

"Well, I hope you thanked her properly."

"I did. You know I wouldn't forget a thing like that."

"Very likely you would forget, Ossie Osgood. I know you only too well. By the way, where's your sports bag? I'd better wash those pyjamas."

"What? Oh, oh, don't worry, they're not dirty, hardly used them. I'll unpack them later. Don't worry, got them all safe in my room."

"That's funny. I didn't see you carrying it when you came home."

"I'm not going again, Mum," said Ossie. "Never going anywhere again. This is the best house in the whole world. And you're the best mum. Give us a cuddle."

Ossie flung himself round his mother's waist and gave her a quick hug, but at that moment the telephone rang. Mrs Osgood untied herself and went to answer it.

"Oh, hello, Grandad. What? Ossie's left his sports bag at your place? What did you say? It's been there all night? Are you sure?"

As she came off the phone, Ossie dashed upstairs.

"Just gotta clear up my room, Mum, I'll make it really neat and tidy, clean everything up, no mess, no dirt, which is how all houses should be . . ."

4

Ossie the Millionaire

Ossie and Desmond were in the playground, arguing, which was what they usually did when they were in the playground.

"Look, over half of them belong to me, so I should get most of the money," said Ossie.

"Yeh, but it was my idea," said Desmond, "so I should get most."

"I'm the entroo-manure, whatever that stupid word is," said Ossie.

"Shurrup," said Dez, "here's some girls."

"Anybody want to buy Co-mics!"

Ossie and Desmond shouted it together, in perfect timing, at the tops of their voices.

Flossie Teacake and her friends hesitated for a second, looked at Ossie and Desmond, then stared down at their pile of rather torn, worn, heavily used copies of *Shoot* and *Roy of the Rovers*. Then each gave a little shudder, and they all walked on, heads in the air.

"No *Dandies* or *Beanos*?" shouted Flossie, turning back to look at them. Ossie and Dez looked at each other, wondering who to blame.

"I suppose you're *still* reading them . . ."

At the lunchtime bell, there was a mad dash for the dinner queue. Ossie and Dez both stayed to dinner, their mothers having paid in advance for tickets for the whole term. They both thought this was very unfair.

"If only they'd give us the money in our hands each week," said Dez. "Yeh, then we could spend it all on Tuck."

Dinner was a choice of stew or salad, which they both hated, but they did manage to force down a good bit of each, then they raced to the Tuck Shop.

It wasn't really a Tuck Shop, just a trestle table set up in a corridor where sixth formers took turns to sell sweets, crisps, soft drinks and cakes, all profits going to the School Fund.

"How much you got?" said Ossie, fighting his

way through the queue, creeping under the legs of bigger boys and girls.

Desmond was a bit taller, but he too managed to get through, dodging the kids trying to kick them, swing bags at them or stand on their hands.

"How much you got then?" said Desmond.

"How much you got?" said Ossie.

"I just asked you that."

They kept up this conversation, pushing and shoving each other as well as other people, till eventually they reached the top of the queue.

"Hurry up, you two berks," said a bossy sixth-form girl.

"Mars Bar, please," said Ossie.

"Same here," said Desmond. "He's paying."

"No, I'm not," said Ossie. "I'm broke."

"I thought you were paying?"

"I thought you were."

The sixth former grabbed back both the Mars Bars, then picked up an empty box and banged Desmond and Ossie over the head. The rest of the queue joined in, pulling and pushing Desmond and Ossie, till they ended up at the back of the queue, where they had begun.

Maths was the last lesson of the day. Naturally enough, Ossie and Desmond, both sitting at the back of the class room, quickly got down to some hard, concentrated study, once Miss Turkey had explained which Algebraic problems she wanted them to work on.

"I'd buy a new car first," said Ossie.

"Same here," said Desmond. "I'd get a Roller. Only a hundred grand."

"A what?" asked Ossie. "That's what painters

use, isn't it? You wouldn't be doing painting and decorating, if you were a millionaire."

"That's what they call a Rolls Royce, dum dum."

"Oh, they're a bit too big. I'd get something neater, like a Posh."

"You mean a Porsche."

"OK, if you want to talk posh—I'd get a Porsh Porsche."

"And as my second car," continued Desmond, "I'd get a BMW."

"Don't think I'd need two cars, even if I was a millionaire," said Ossie.

"Yeh, you can only drive one at a time."

"Heh, but how about getting a Sinclair C 5, those little electric ones. I'd like one for indoor use, to take me round my enormous house."

"Oh yeh," said Desmond. "Forgot about a house. I'd have a whopper, with a TV in every room, including the toilet."

"And a swimming pool, a gym, and a snooker table."

"I've already got a snooker table," said Desmond.

"Huh," said Ossie, "call that cardboard thing a snooker table. Crappy rubbish."

"Right, Osgood, that's the last time you get invited to my house."

"Wouldn't need to go to your house, if I was a millionaire. I'd have a proper snooker room, with a full-sized slate table . . ."

"I'd get a new computer," said Desmond thoughtfully. "Mine's almost three months old now."

Ossie, who lived in a computer-less, Walkman-less, snooker-less house, ignored this remark. When it came to electrical equipment, Desmond seemed to have most of the exciting, modern inventions this world can offer. Or so he said.

"I think I'd go for a Midi System and a Personal Stereo," said Desmond. "Either Dolby Dee or Bang and Olafsen. With Tweeters, of course."

"Really," said Ossie, very impressed.

"And Woofers. Hopeless without Woofers."

"That's true," said Ossie, thinking hard of something equally impressive. No point in being a millionaire, unless you know the best stuff to waste your money on.

"Heh, I saw this brill remote-controlled radio car the other day in this shop," said Ossie. "Can't quite remember the name, or the number, but it was only a hundred and thirty-three pounds. Looked well smart. Really lush. Mass doss."

Ossie had now used up all his slang, and all his technical knowledge.

"I thought it was you two," said Miss Turkey, suddenly appearing beside their desk, "making all that noise. Right. I want to see your work book, Osgood. At once."

Ossie had been scribbling and doodling during his chat with Desmond, without really thinking about it. It was a bit messy, with drawings and scribbles and crossings out, but he slowly held it out for inspection by Miss.

1 RR plus 1 BMW = £150,000 wot will P be.

Miss Turkey studied these strange words and figures for some time.

"Yes, I suppose I can see your rough workings out," she said. "Your handwriting is becoming impossible, though. Just make sure you copy it out neatly in your homework book. And please check those letters. I think you'll find it's X and Y we are looking for in that question. Right, there's the bell. Class dismissed."

Ossie was walking slowly home from school, another day over, and deeper in debt. He'd managed to wheedle twenty pence out of Flossie Teacake and had bought himself an ice lolly. She wanted the money back first thing on Monday, or else.

"She's so mean," said Ossie. "And what does she mean, 'Or Else'? Is she threatening me, or does she mean Elsie Parsnip in 1G. I've already tried her. She's broke as well."

Ossie knew it was unfair to expect any more money from his mother, as she had such a hard struggle to run the house, all on her own, and her part-time job didn't pay much. They didn't have the money coming into their house the way they had at Desmond's, with his dad and two brothers all working.

"But a pound a week. It's ridiculous. One cheap comic, one packet of crisps, one small bar of chocolate, and that's it. It's like being in prison. If only I was eighteen, I could get a proper job, make some real money. It's not fair. This is when I need the money, now, not when I'm eighteen.

"I think I'll go on strike. I'll withdraw my labour, that'll teach them. Only trouble is, I got no labour to withdraw."

"Hi, Mum, it's me. I'm home."

"I wondered who it was," said his mother from the kitchen. "You always come in so quietly, I often think it must be a mouse."

Ossie had fallen over a newspaper, one of those free ones, shoved through the front-door letter-box.

"Not my fault. Someone left a trap for me. I've hurt my leg."

Mrs Osgood and Lucy were making a cake. Ossie often helped, as he did cookery at school.

"Sorry I can't help you," said Ossie. "I think me leg's broken."

"We don't need your leg to make a cake," said Lucy. "You stir it with a spoon, not your big toe."

"Ha ha," said Ossie. "Actually, it's very sore.

As if I haven't got enough problems."

"Such as," said his mother, taking no notice of him.

"Poverty," said Ossie. "It's crippling me."

"As well as your leg," said Lucy.

"Look, you just shurrup. This is serious . . ."

"Hey, you two," said their mother.

"I've just got to get a job," said Ossie.

"Have you considered being a brain surgeon, Ossie?" said Lucy. "Or signing on for your precious Spurs?"

"I've warned you," said Ossie. "One more smart remark . . ."

"I do sympathize, Ossie," said his mother. "But at twelve, you're not legally allowed to do proper jobs, though it is wonderful what you do for Grandad. He really appreciates that."

Ossie wasn't sure if this was sarcasm or not, but he chose to ignore it.

"I wish they'd never stopped children going up chimneys," said Ossie. "I could have done that. I'm just the size. Or sending them down coal mines on their hands and knees to pull horses along. I've always loved animals."

"I don't think they pulled horses," said his mother. "Little trolleys perhaps."

"There you are then," said Ossie. "I do that all the time. Those trolleys in Tesco's are murder. I bet little weedy Victorian kids couldn't pull any of them. Not fair. Stopping good jobs that kids used to have. We did all that in History last week. I told Miss it was stupid. She said it was exploitation. I said *this* is victimization, that's what."

"Would you like to lick the bowl, Ossie?" said his mother.

"Or are you slimming?" said Lucy. She quickly ducked out of the way before Ossie could hit her with his Spurs bag.

"If I can't get a job," said Ossie, "I want double my allowance."

"You do me your sums, itemize exactly what you spend it on, prepare proper accounts, then I might consider it."

"Oh God, you sound just like Miss Turkey. I come home to get away from her."

"Don't say Oh God," said his mother. "Your grandad doesn't like it."

"Wasn't me. It was Poverty talking."

"I think you do jolly well. I buy all your clothes, pay your fares, clubs, school things. All you have to spend your money on is your own pleasure."

"Yeh, but pleasures come dear these days, Mum. You're still living in the Sixties. Do you know how much a Rolls Royce is today?"

"Amaze me," said his mother.

"Desmond says at least a hundred thousand pounds. How am I going to get that sort of money, on a pound a week? I'll be, hold on, let me think, one thousand years old before I can afford one."

"That was quick working out, Ossie. Your Maths lessons have not been in vain."

"Actually, Mum," said Lucy, "there are fifty-two weeks in a year. So at a pound a week, that's fifty-two pounds a year. It will only take him till he's nine hundred and sixty years old . . ."

"Listen, Einstein," said Ossie, "go back to sleep, eh. Just grunt when you're spoken to."

"Have you considered," said his mother, "taking some money out of your bank accounts? It might be enough to go towards, well, perhaps a second-hand Rolls Royce . . ."

Ossie at that moment held three accounts, which he had been moving around recently to take advantage of any free gifts. So far, he'd got a Lloyds wallet, a sports bag from the Midland, and the Anglia Building Society Junior Account had promised him a birthday card.

"How much have you got in altogether, Ossie?" said Lucy.

"I think, hold on, not counting the interest, about, let me see, perhaps nineteen pounds ninety pence altogether. I'll just go and get my bank books."

Ossie jumped up to run upstairs. He was in such a hurry that once again he tripped over the newspaper, still lying behind the front door.

As he lay on the doormat, groaning, he noticed a leaflet which had fallen out of the newspaper. NEWSBOYS AND GIRLS WANTED TO DELIVER NEWSPAPERS.

Ossie was on his feet in an instant, running back across the living room, straight for the telephone.

"Perhaps you *are* going to be asked to join Spurs,

Ossie," said Lucy. "It could be the Chief Scout."

She was peeping through the front-window curtains, observing two men in very smart suits, each carrying a briefcase, who were standing at the front door.

"We've come about Master Osgood's job application," said one of them as Mrs Osgood opened the door. He said he was the *Post*'s Circulation Manager.

Mrs Osgood invited them both in and called upstairs for Ossie. He had been watching from his bedroom window.

They each had clipboards and solemnly handed various documents to Ossie. One was marked "Job Description", another "Company Policy". Ossie glanced at them all very quickly, but he slowed down at one called "Disciplinary Code".

It warned that any newsboy or newsgirl caught not delivering the papers to the required number of houses, would be penalized. But even worse, the crime of dumping the aforesaid newspapers would result in instant dismissal.

"Yeh, seems OK," mumbled Ossie.

"Now, Rates of Pay," said the Circulation

Manager, clearing his throat. "We are currently paying two pence per paper, but should we rise above a hundred pages, and we sincerely intend to, then it will be three pence. Is that clear?"

Ossie nodded. He was feeling quite excited.

"We estimate, therefore, that your rate of delivery should result in a payment of one pound seventy-six an hour. Not bad, is it Mrs Osgood, for a young gentleman of thirteen years of age?"

Ossie looked worried. He had already been working out how many Mars Bars a week could be bought for one pound seventy-six, or how many decades it would take for a Rolls Royce.

"You are thirteen, are you? Hmm? You know the rules of the land. Our company could never connive at the employment of minors."

"I'm as good as thirteen," began Ossie. "In fact I know thirteen-year-olds who are really titchy. You should see some of the kids in our school . . ."

"Actually," said his mother, "he will be thirteen in just five weeks."

"Oh, in that case," said the younger executive, "nao problema."

"Yes," said the manager, "we can start off with

you, Mrs Osgood, officially being the newspaper boy, I mean newspaper girl, sorry about the sexist remark, har har har. You are over thirteen, are you? Har, har, har. Then after five weeks, your big strapping son, where is he, oh there he is, hee hee hee, crouching again, he can then take over the round from you."

"And in the meantime," said the executive, with a big wink, "young Oswald can of course be 'helping' you. Get my drift. Say no more?"

"The first delivery will arrive here on Monday evening at four o'clock," said the manager, "just as you come home from school."

On Monday, Ossie ran all the way home from school, possibly for the first time in his life.

He was breathless when he reached his gate and began to worry that his asthma might come on. Not just because of the unaccustomed running, but the excitement of being an Employed Person.

He also felt a bit sick. On the strength of his one pound seventy-six a week, still unearned, he'd borrowed from Flossie. He had had two Mars Bars at lunchtime, to build up his strength for his Big Job, or so he explained.

On the doorstep, as arranged, was a very large bundle of newspapers, plus an enormous fluorescent orange newspaper bag.

Both Mrs Osgood and Lucy helped Ossie to load up his bag. They helped him get it on to his back and stood back to admire. Ossie fell down.

Lucy burst out laughing, but Mrs Osgood gave her one of her looks.

"I'll tell you what," said his mother. "Just do half first of all. Leave the rest here, and come back later. It's bound to take you time to get used to it. You'll be using muscles you've never used before."

"You mean muscles I haven't got," said Ossie, staggering out of the gate, then falling down again.

It took Ossie ages and ages to get the first half delivered. When he eventually crawled back almost on his knees he found his mother had kindly been out and delivered the other half.

Ossie then went straight to bed, absolutely exhausted, without having his tea.

On the following Monday, Ossie was kept in after

school. It wasn't his fault. Everyone in the class had been talking, messing about, larking around, but only Ossie had been caught and punished.

When he got home, both Lucy and his mother were out.

"Trust them," said Ossie, "just when I need them."

He was about to make himself a cup of tea before starting, when he saw the *Post*'s delivery van come down his street.

"Oh no, that could be the Inspector. They do random checks, just to make sure all the papers get delivered."

It was dark before he had finished, by which time he was not only exhausted but very frightened. He had staggered into some bushes, not being able to see his way, then walked into a garden pond.

One woman had screamed at him, saying she was going to call the police, because she thought he was a burglar. Another one said she was calling her solicitor if one more free newspaper was shoved through her letterbox without her written permission.

★

On the third Monday, Ossie's delivery round lasted in all four hours. Three of them were spent in the casualty department of the local hospital.

It wasn't Ossie's fault, of course. He was getting on with his work as best he could, arguing with his conscience about the morality of dumping just a small quantity of the free newspaper.

"If some people don't want them, what's the point of delivering them? It's bad for the company image if people hate the company. So I'm helping the company not to be hated. Stands to reason."

At that moment, unseen by Ossie, a large Afghan hound came out of the side of a large house. Ossie was on the front step stretching up to deliver another *Post*.

The dog did not actually attack Ossie, so the owner later claimed. It was just being friendly.

It was probably Ossie himself who scared the dog, turning round so suddenly when he felt what appeared to be human hands on the back of his shoulders. He found himself face to face with what he then thought was an enormous bear, standing over him, about to eat him. He let out such a

scream that the dog was terrified, grabbed Ossie's
ankle, and they both fell down the steps.

'Mrs Osgood decided that Ossie should have a
tetanus injection, just in case the dog had bitten
him.

On the fourth Monday, Ossie asked his mother to
do the round for him, pleading industrial injuries,
plus pressure of homework.

"That's the first time in my life I've ever heard
you say that," said his mother.

"Then after that, Mum, I'll have to do my violin practice."

"Another world first."

"Anyway, my ankle's still sore and I'm too tired."

"You're just too lazy, if you ask me," said Lucy.

"No, I'm just too small. I'll always be like this. I know it. I'm stuck with this stupid body."

"All right then," said his mother. "Just this once. I'll do it for you."

"Thanks, Mum," said Ossie, lying down on the sofa. "I don't think I could have been a chimney sweep after all . . ."

There was no fifth Monday delivery of free newspapers to the Osgood residence. Ossie said that he couldn't manage it any longer.

Mrs Osgood had refused point blank to do them again. So that was that. She rang the Circulation Manager. She had fulfilled her part of the contract. Her son was cancelling his. Terribly sorry. Pressure of school work.

"At least I paid off my debts," said Ossie. "I don't owe that Flossie or Dez anything now."

"So how much have you made altogether, Ossie?" asked Lucy.

"Absolutely nothing. I'm back where I started. Broke. I think I might as well just go to bed and sleep till I'm eighteen . . ."

Eighteen-year-old Oz came out of his grandfather's bedroom. Once again, he had put on the magical belt and shot up immediately in age.

This time, his grandfather was not at home, which was unusual, but then Brookfield School had finished early, because of a staff meeting. Grandad had perhaps gone to pick up his pension.

Oz left the flat and headed for the Job Centre in the High Street. After that he might have a look at a private Employment Agency. They would all be rushing to offer him something, now that he was such a big, strong eighteen-year-old, eager and willing to do anything, go anywhere.

"I might make, oh I dunno, probably twenty pounds a day, plus overtime, bonuses, incentives, perhaps luncheon vouchers as well. I wonder if they give share options to eighteen-year-olds?"

He was in the High Street in a very short time, but then with big, strong, eighteen-year-old legs, and people on the pavements getting out of your way, you do move pretty quickly.

Oz was going past an alleyway which he knew well, between a builder's yard and a printing works, when an old man staggered out, looking very flustered, carrying a large case.

"Can I help you, sir?" enquired Oz, solicitously.

The man looked startled. He wasn't quite as old as Oz had imagined, nowhere near Grandad's age, but he did look rather worn and hunted.

"No, no, thanks," said the man. "It's not heavy. Thank you."

Oz did not recognize the man's accent, but he could tell it wasn't local.

Oz paused to watch the man get safely across the street, just in case he did need assistance, and then he continued on his way up the High Street, whistling merrily. At twelve, he could hardly whistle anything, merrily or otherwise.

"Perhaps I'll get a job helping old people. Even carrying old people, as I'm so strong. Digging their gardens. Building houses for them. When you're eighteen, you can do anything."

★

Oz was so busy thinking about possible jobs, whistling his merriest tunes, that he didn't at first hear a commotion behind him. This was followed by a lot of shouting and cars braking. Oz turned round to find that the old man he'd tried to help now lay sprawled on the pavement.

About fifty metres further on, charging his way through the crowds, was a tall man wearing a balaclava helmet. He was carrying some sort of instrument in one hand, and the old man's case in the other. In a flash, Oz was after him. Oz didn't bother to keep on the pavement, but ran straight down the middle of the road and quickly caught up thirty metres. Then, while still ten metres away, Oz brought the mugger down with a brilliant rugby tackle, getting him round the ankles, as you're supposed to, so that you do little damage to yourself. The man fell to the ground, hitting the pavement hard, and lay there apparently unconscious.

Oz was quickly on his feet, hardly out of breath. He looked around for the case which had gone flying through the air and had landed inside a shop doorway. It was an old-fashioned, very battered case, but securely locked, so it hadn't opened.

Oz went into the shop where all the assistants had been watching the incident, absolutely astounded. They gave Oz a cheer and congratulated him, asking if he was all right.

Oz had wasted a few moments in the shop, retrieving the case. As he came out a beat-up old Jaguar was screeching away from the pavement, the door still half open, with the mugger, looking very dazed, being pulled inside.

Even Oz thought it would be hard to race a Jaguar sports car.

He might be able to catch it up, being eighteen and a mile champion, but then one of the muggers might have a gun. So he ran back down the High Street with the case.

The old man was still lying on the same spot, surrounded by people trying to help him, saying he should call an ambulance or ring for the police.

"Oh thank, thank, thank you," he said when he saw Oz with his case. His gnarled face showed immense relief, though not much of a smile.

"I'll take you to hospital myself if you like," said Oz. "Here, get on my back."

But the old man had staggered to his feet and took the case from Oz.

"No need, no need. I'm so late now. Got urgent plane to catch. Must go now."

He started off down the street again, rather shakily, so Oz walked with him, helping with the case, and holding the man's arm.

"I'll report it to the police," said Oz. "Save you doing it . . ."

"Oh, don't do that," said the old man, suddenly stopping, a look of panic in his eyes.

He pulled Oz into an alleyway, saying he had something for him. He turned his back to the street, got out some keys and slowly opened the case, trying not to let Oz see what was inside. Being a polite and well-brought-up eighteen-year-old, Oz took the hint and tried not to look, but he did catch sight of what seemed to be piles and piles of coloured paper.

"Here, take this," the man said to Oz. "For helping me."

The man started shoving wads and wads of notes into Oz's hands, into his pockets, into his shirt, down his jeans, so that very soon Oz seemed to be covered completely in money.

"Please, please, one thing only. No need to go to the police. I am OK. You have saved the money. And I have rewarded you. You can now forget it, so?"

He gave Oz a smile, the first Oz had noticed.

The old man gave a quick shout and stopped a taxi. He climbed in while Oz was still trying to work out exactly what happened.

"I'll have the biggest Knickerbocker Glory you have," said Oz. "With double cream, special chocolate sauce, extra bananas, peaches, the full treatment. Thank you. And make it snappy, I'll probably be having seconds later."

The waitress in the ice-cream parlour had not taken much notice of Oz at first. But in taking his order, she clearly saw that he was counting a bundle of twenty-pound notes. Her eyes practically popped. She hurried to tell the manager.

"Hmm," said Oz to himself. "I'm not quite sure if I am a millionaire. I keep on forgetting how many I've got to. Now, is that bundle ten thousand or twenty thousand pounds? Oh, well, I'll have to start again."

When the Knickerbocker arrived, Oz gave the girl a large tip and asked her to bring him a pencil and a large carrier bag.

The manager himself brought them, insisting that Oz had a free Biro, compliments of the management, and a large carrier bag on the side of which was printed "Marine Ices".

"How much?" said Oz.

"No, no, it's a present. It will be good for Marine Ices to have such a wealthy, I mean, valued customer as your good self walking round advertising our establishment."

"Oh, thanks," said Oz.

"And might I suggest that you try one of our specialities, either the Surprise Bombe or the Vesuvius, the Anacleto Delight or even Dante's Infernal Super Ice? All on the house, of course. We just want to know what you think of them, as a young man of obvious wealth, I mean obvious good taste."

Oz decided to try all four, just to be helpful, then he worried that he might be getting fat.

"I suppose that is a problem about being a millionaire. You can eat too much of a good thing.

Never thought about that before.

"I've also discovered another thing. When you have money, people want to give you things for free. When you're poor, you get nothing for free. Funny world."

Oz was causing what looked like pandemonium in Dixon's Super Store. Every assistant was rushing back and forward, bringing out bigger and better calculators, computers, TV sets, stereos, Walkmen, video cameras, video games.

"Yes, yes, I'll take that, and that, and this, and have you got that in red? Good, I'll take three."

The counter was piled so high with Oz's purchases that they had to start a new pile in the middle of the shop.

"And what about Twitters and Tweeters, Wipers and Weepers, Poofers and Doofers. Must have them. Don't want Desmond to think I'm one of those millionaires who doesn't know anything."

"Poofers, sir?" said one of the assistants.

"Yes, I used to be an ignoramus like you, when I was a little boy. I'll excuse you this time. Just get me everything. I'm paying. You're working."

Oz put his hand in his carrier bag, as if it was a lucky dip, and flashed one of his bundles. At once, the assistant darted away. He teetered back with boxes reaching almost to the ceiling.

"Would sir like them delivered?" asked the manager, hovering in the background.

"Well, I can't carry all of them, can I?" said Oz. "I've not got my Roller yet, have I? Just send them to my home. But I'll pay now. What's the damage, squire?"

Oz whistled and looked bored while a conference was held on Oz's bill. It came to £29,999.99.

"Funny how everything in electrical shops always comes to something ending in ninety-nine pence."

Oz peeled off £30,000 in fifty-pound notes, and told the manager to keep the change.

"So you've done pretty well," said Oz, as the assistant took the one penny. "I know that rich people usually ask for a discount. I happen to be rather an eccentric millionaire. Cheers!"

Things were more subdued in the car showroom,

but then motor salesmen are more used to people coming in with a lot of cash and wanting to buy a new car.

It was a bit unusual, though, to have someone clearly only eighteen who was asking about both a Rolls Royce and a Porsche, plus a Sinclair C 5 for domestic evening use. The latter was going to be a trifle difficult to acquire as it was a discontinued line.

"While we ring a few contacts," said a very smooth salesman in a striped suit, "would sir like a little run?"

"No thanks," said Oz. "I've eaten too much ice-cream."

"Jolly witty, sir. I mean in the Silver Spirit or perhaps the Corniche?"

"Yeh, of course," said Oz. "I'll have a trial ride. I don't want to get it home and find the cocktail cabinet's too titchy."

The salesman drove the Rolls at first, then naturally wanted Oz to try it for himself, to feel the immaculate suspension, listen to the silence.

Oz hesitated for a moment, not knowing if he

would manage. But he remembered he was eighteen, able to do almost anything. And with fully automatic transmission and power-assisted steering, driving was remarkably easy.

"Any child could drive this," said Oz. "Any common or garden millionaire's child, of course."

Oz thought about taking the Rolls Royce out in the countryside, to get on the motorway and really test it, but he decided he might still want a run in a Porsche, perhaps try a few other trifles.

On the way back through town, he did manage to get the speedometer up to 50 mph. The salesman in his stiff suit fiddled nervously with the rose in his buttonhole, worrying that he might lose this obviously rich prospective customer if he told him off for breaking the speed limit.

The car suddenly juddered to a halt as Oz jammed on the brakes.

"Just testing," said Oz. "I can now hear the car clock ticking over."

"Yes, that is one of our boasts," said the salesman.

"I say, old man, could you be a sport and get out

and open those big gates over there," said Oz. "Thanks awfully."

Driving a posh car was making Oz talk in a posh way: just as throwing his money around in a flash manner had made him talk and act flash.

"This isn't your house, is it, sir?" said the salesman.

"Not yet, though I might make an offer. At the moment it's my school, I mean my old school. I used to come here, oh many months ago."

Oz had not realized till he was almost past that he was so near the back gates of Brookfield School.

On the football pitch, an after-school game of football was going on. In the girls' playground, they were practising netball.

Everyone stopped, both the boys and the girls, when they saw a brand new Rolls Royce driving into the school playground.

"Hiya fans," yelled Oz, banging on the window.

"Allow me, sir," said the salesman, pressing a button. Immediately the windows slid down.

"Thanks, squire," said Oz. "Anyone wanna ride? How about you, Craigy baby? You look a bit knackered to me. Jump in and I'll drive you to the penalty area. You were always a bit slow."

Craig, captain of the Under 13 team, looked amazed that anyone should know his name, let alone his speed problems.

Oz then did a three-point turn, very quickly, making the tyres screech, and drew up beside the netball pitch.

"Too many Mars Bars, Flossie, that's your problem, my petal."

Flossie had started to play again, and was about to shoot a goal, but dropped it the minute she heard her name being called.

"Right, if you'd all like to queue up in a neat line," shouted Oz, getting out of his seat and standing on the roof of the Rolls. "I'm about to give out twenty-pound notes to certain people, but only if I like the look of them, only if they've been nice to me. I mean if they look nice to me . . ."

There was immediately a massive scramble, as about fifty boys and girls left the playing areas and rushed to the Rolls.

"Do be careful, sir," said the salesman. "We

shouldn't like any scratches."

"Don't worry, my old son," said Oz. "I'll pay for any damages."

Oz handed out twenty-pound notes to almost everyone, all except those who had been horrible to him in the past.

"You, boy, I'm told you often do a bit of bullying, especially of younger, weedier boys. I'm only allowing you ten pounds. There could be more another time, depending on your good conduct."

"Oh, thanks very much, very good of you, I will try."

"I didn't realize I had any tenners left," said Oz, putting his hand into one of his pockets. "Such silly little notes. Not worth keeping. What can you buy with a tenner these days?"

Oz then started throwing tenners up in the air, watching them float down. They were at once fought over by all the school children, pushing and shoving each other, fighting and kicking to get most.

In the far corner of the playground, a door opened, and out came Mr Bott and Miss Turkey, followed by about another fifty teachers. They had finally finished their staff meeting and were rushing to get their cars and go home.

Oz jumped off the car roof, to get back into the Rolls, in case he might be recognized.

The staff stood for a moment, transfixed by the sight. Suddenly, they all started running towards Oz and the Rolls. They threw themselves on the pile of bodies, squabbling with the children for the ten-pound notes.

"Heh you fatso," said Oz to Mr Bott. "There are conditions attached to my enormous generosity."

Oz stretched into the writhing mass and pulled Botty out by the ankles. Being eighteen, and very strong, it was no problem.

"No hitting boys with that slipper from now on," said Oz. "Especially first years. No rope climbing, no forward rolls and no showers for anyone who does not want them. Is that clear?"

"Oh yes, if you say so."

"Ah, Miss Turkey, I'm told you're a rather caring teacher," said Oz. "Just try and care a bit better in future for one or two of your smaller charges, especially with lessons like Maths. Pay them more attention, and give better marks.

"Never ever shout at them again or tell them off, especially ones called Ossie . . . Are you listening? Good, in that case I might be able to find some fifty-pound notes just for you."

Oz turned out all his pockets, in his trousers and jacket, looked up his sleeves and in his shirt, and threw the last of his loose money in the air. He still had the carrier bag, with a great deal left in.

"Cheerio, peasants," he shouted, getting back into the car. "Be good. Bye-ee. Home, James . . ."

Oz let the salesman drive back to the showroom at a leisurely pace.

He was wondering why he hadn't noticed Desmond. He'd boasted he'd been picked for the Under 13's, but there had been no sign of him in the playground.

"I wonder if I should buy my own team. How much do you think Spurs would cost, driver?" said Oz.

"You're a horse rider, are you, sir?"

"Yes, I'll probably buy a few horses as well, just to amuse my little sister. Heh, stop, driver. I think I know that deprived little person over there."

The driver stopped and Oz pressed the button for the electrically operated window. He shouted out at what appeared to be a small orange splodge in the distance.

"Hey, boy, would you like a lift?"

The orange splodge was resting beside a gate, sorting out something on the pavement.

"Just drive along the pavement," said Oz to the driver. "Go on, I'll pay any fines. When you're a millionaire, you don't mind breaking rules."

Desmond almost jumped out of his skin. The Rolls Royce pulled to a halt, just two inches from his foot.

"Jump in, Dez, old son," said Oz. "I'll help you deliver those boring papers. You look well tired."

"How do you know my name?" asked Desmond. "Who's been talking to you?"

"This has," said Oz, flashing a bundle of notes. "Money talks."

Desmond got into the car and Oz drove him from

gate to gate. Very soon Desmond was exhausted once again. So Oz picked up both the bag and Desmond, and carried them along each front path. In the end, Oz finished the job himself. Being eighteen, he was round in a trice.

"You should always help people smaller than yourself," said Oz. "And if you have more possessions than other people, such as a snooker table, however cheap, or the latest computer game, you should let your less well-off friends play with them first, and let them have the best cues and the best bats."

"Oh yes, I'll try to from now on."

"Right, let me drive you home. It's that high-rise block over there, isn't it?"

"How did you know?" asked Dez.

"I know everything."

Desmond relaxed in the back of the car, touching all the leather, examining the telephones and the fridge.

"Put on the tele if you like," said Oz. "I think it's a children's programme now, so you'll like that."

Oz opened the last copy of the paper, which had somehow been left over from Desmond's round. In the Stop Press column was a big headline.

COUNTERFEITER IN HIGH STREET MUGGING INCIDENT DRAMA

There were not many details, as the news was still coming in, but it said that the messenger for an international counterfeit gang had been attacked by a mugger while leaving a printing works. He had escaped, but a large quantity of the counterfeit money had been scattered in the High Street. A lot of it had been handed to the police, but several people had tried to cash it, believing it to be real. The police were now guarding all airports, but it was feared the messenger might already be abroad.

"I think we'll get off here," said Oz suddenly. "Out you get Desmond, you lazy thing."

"What about the car?" said the salesman. "You're still keen, aren't you?"

"Oh yeh, very keen," said Oz, getting out. "But don't ring me, I'll ring you. It's just that I prefer to walk home."

"Very good, sir," said the salesman. "Oh, and

here's your carrier bag. Can't forget that, can we, sir . . ."

Oz was quite out of breath by the time he reached his grandad's home. He'd run all the way, still carrying his carrier bag.

"I can't dump it, can I? I could be had up for a litter offence."

He crept round the back of the Sheltered Housing block to a little garden where he knew old Ma Pigg, one of Grandad's neighbours, had an incinerator. It was still smouldering.

Oz emptied his bagful of notes on to the embers. He bent down and blew and blew. Eventually, it burst into flames.

"All that money, up in flames," said Oz, watching till the last embers had gone. "Good job I didn't bring anything home. Nobody's been cheated out of any goods. Except that Knickerbocker Glory. I'll pay them back, one of these decades."

Oz crept into his grandad's flat, put the belt safely away in the wardrobe for another day, if there ever was going to be another day. He was then transformed once more back into his twelve-year-old self.

Ossie stood in the hall and listened. There was no television noise, but of course that didn't mean his grandad's TV was off. He could hear some talking, so he opened the living-room door, very quietly.

"I'll be in tomorrow, if you want to come here," his grandfather was saying. "Yes, I filled in the form. You'll have to bring home the what? The Terms of Employment, the Disciplinary Code, and the Job Description? That sounds a queer old clart."

The voice at the other end was obviously puzzled by Grandad's northern slang. Ossie half wanted to come in and explain to whoever was on the end of the line.

". . . nothing, nothing," continued Grandad. "Right then, I'll be here tomorrow. Where do I go?"

Ossie heard his grandfather hang up. He then banged at the front door, as if he'd just arrived.

"Hello, Grandad," said Ossie, coming into the

143

living room. "Was that you on the phone?"

"Could have been," said Grandad. "You haven't been spying on me, have you?"

"No, just thought I heard you talking to someone as I came in."

"I can talk, can't I? Not a law against talking. You young kids think you can do everything in this world."

"Some older kids can," said Ossie. "I can't. I'm not allowed to do anything worth doing."

"I might be getting a job," said Grandad. "Not a word to anyone, not to your mum, and certainly not that old bat Ma Pigg."

"What sort of work, Grandad?"

"Highly secret work. I have to sign the Official Secrets Act, and other important documents . . ."

"Did they ask your age?"

"I just said I was over eighteen. Which I am. That's all that matters, don't you worry yourself, my lad."

"Yeh, you're lucky, Grandad. Wish I was eighteen."

"You will be. Just stop going on about it. Now go and put that kettle on . . ."